NEWPORT PAGNELL

A Pictorial History

High Street, Newport Pagnell, *c.*1900.

NEWPORT PAGNELL

A Pictorial History

Dennis Mynard and Julian Hunt

Phillimore

1995

Published by
PHILLIMORE & CO. LTD.,
Shopwyke Manor Barn, Chichester, West Sussex
in association with
Buckinghamshire County Library

ISBN 0 85033 995 2

Printed and bound in Great Britain by
BIDDLES LTD.
Guildford, Surrey

List of Illustrations

Acknowledgements

Many of the photographs used in this book have been collected over the years by Dennis Mynard and other members of the Newport Pagnell Historical Society. Many more are from the County Reference Library and the County Museum whose collections are currently being digitised and will soon be available on compact disc at the Museum and at several of the county's libraries. Where illustrations are not separately acknowledged, they are from the County Reference Library. The photographs numbered 27, 29, 76, 95-6 and 118 are from the County Museum. Buckinghamshire County Record Office supplied illustrations 28, 94 and 114, whilst item 144 is from Northamptonshire Record Office.

The Royal Commission on the Historical Monuments of England, whose photographic collections are now housed at Swindon, has supplied copies of a survey of Newport Pagnell made in 1967 by Ray Bailey. RCHM photographs are numbered 19, 23, 36, 47-8, 52, 54, 73, 77, 81, 97-9, 101, 107, 110, 113, 117, 119, 124-5, 129, 131-2, 134, 138, 141, 143, 153-4, 158, 160 and 168. Newport Pagnell Historical Society photographs are numbered 20, 121, 126, 133, 139, 147, 155, 163-4. Numbers 8, 11-13, 18, 24, 32, 58, 61, 74, 83, 87-9, 93, 105-6, 108, 116, 123, 127, 130, 135-7, 142, 146, 149, 151, 161-2, 167, 171 are from Dennis Mynard's own collection.

Mr. J.H. Venn of Great Missenden has contributed his own photographs (5, 46, 59, 67-8, 75, 102-3, 128 and 148) and one taken by the late Stanley Freese (9); Mr. A.J. Petford took photographs 44-5. Other photographs were loaned by Kit Clare (112), Shaun Higgins (165-6), Richard Odell (80), Cliff Petts (104, 150, 152, 156-7), Ted Platt (85), Michael Pratt (21-2, 30-1, 63, 109, 120, 145, 159). The authors are grateful to Janet Robinson and Joan Chibnall for permission to reproduce sketch maps, to Valerie West for illustrations 64-6 and 69-72, which are from her 1974 thesis, and to Sir Philip Duncombe for allowing the use of the drawing numbered 62.

Introduction

Newport Pagnell is a classic example of an English market town—a place where farmers sell their produce, travellers break their journeys, and townspeople help them to spend their money. The first reference to a market anywhere in Buckinghamshire is in 1187 when Gervase Pagnell gave the monks of Tickford Priory the right to buy provisions free of toll in the market of Newport. Many towns proudly preserve market charters of much later date in their museums but Newport obviously had a market long before kings thought of selling market rights to boost their revenues. 'Port' is an old word for a market, but we can only guess when Newport's market was new.

Early History

Gravel extraction in modern times has revealed ample evidence that the Ouse and Ousel valleys were settled as long ago as 2,000 B.C. and that the area supported a substantial agricultural population in Roman times. Gravel digging near the Sherington Road produced a Bronze-Age collared urn of c.1000 B.C. and a burial mound survived in the Bury Field until levelled by ploughing as part of the war effort in 1939. Local historian Alfred Bullard, writing in 1946, recorded that 'four portions of a burial urn have been found on the high ground above St. John Street near the Church'.

A small farmstead of the late Iron Age dating from the 1st century B.C. was located during gravel working in the Sherington Road pits, where finds included pottery shards and a quern stone. A similar site was found in 1926 at Lodge Farm on the Crawley Road and another near the Ouse on the north side of Little Linford Lane is known from aerial photography.

An excavation in the gardens of Tickford Abbey revealed a minor Roman settlement dating from the 2nd-4th centuries A.D. During the development of the Green Park Estate to the west of the town, an ornate silver ligula was found. A ligula is a long narrow object like a spoon, used by Roman women to extract make-up from a container. Another find from the Roman period, a gold bracelet in the form of a snake, was sold to the British Museum by the vicar of Newport in the last century. There is no indication of any early settlement in the centre of the town although Roman coins have been found in gardens in the High Street and Caldecote Street.

The pagan-Saxon peoples who came to this country after the Roman occupation settled extensively in the Ouse and Ousel valleys during the 5th-7th centuries. Within the parish of Newport Pagnell there are three known Saxon cemeteries suggesting that there are nearby settlements as yet undiscovered. One of the cemeteries was located in 1900 during gravel digging behind the Union Workhouse on London Road. Several burials were found along with an assortment of Saxon objects including two swords, a spearhead, an iron-bound bucket, simple jewellery and an elaborate late-Roman glass beaker of Rhenish origin. Another cemetery was found in the 1920s during gravel digging east of Tickford Abbey. Several burials were said to have grave goods including swords, spears and pottery and the then owner of Tickford Abbey, Dr. Douglas Morris, gave two Saxon pots to the British Museum. The third cemetery was found near Kickles Farm in the 1840s. A sword from one of the graves was given to Wisbech Museum by a farmer who had moved to that area.

The stray find in the High Street of a coin of Offa, King of Mercia from 757-796, does not necessarily prove an early Saxon settlement here and the founding of the present town is probably much later. In the late 9th century, Watling Street formed the boundary between Saxon Mercia and the eastern part of the country under Danish control. King Alfred took London from the Danes in 885 and the subsequent treaty moved the border, so that Newport would then have been on the Saxon side. This could explain why in Domesday Book, Newport and the surrounding settlements are described in a variety of Saxon and Danish measures. Whichever side first fortified the high ground at the junction of the Ouse with the Lovat, it would be to secure a convenient river crossing point during these troubled times. The market or 'port' would have been planned by the Saxons in much the same way as the town of Buckingham was laid out next to the early 10th-century castle there. The site of Newport's castle is just to the east of the cemetery lodge in the old church yard between the Ouse and the Lovat. The field to the south of the river is still called the Castle Meadow.

Domesday Book

In Domesday Book, Newport Pagnell is simply 'Newport'. Before the Conquest it had belonged to Ulf, a thegn of King Edward, but by 1086 William son of Ansculf de Picquigny was the owner. This Norman overlord held land in 12 counties and had Dudley Castle as his principal stronghold. Newport and Buckingham are the only Buckinghamshire towns in Domesday Book afforded the status of a borough. The principal inhabitants of a borough were called 'burgesses' and paid a small rent in cash for their houses, as against 'villeins' (tenants in villages) who cultivated the lord of the manor's land as part of their rent. The burgesses' houses were usually laid out in rows either side of a market place. In the case of Newport, 'burgage plots' were arranged east to west along the High Street with those on the north side having back gates on the aptly named 'Dung Hill Lane' (later modified to Dungeon Lane and now called Union Street). On a map or aerial photograph it is apparent that these plots are not straight but have an 's' shaped curve. This has led some historians to suggest that Newport's burgage plots were laid out on the lines of ploughing ridges in the former open fields. Domesday Book does not say how many burgesses there were in Newport, but there are over 20 burgage plots between the High Street and Union Street alone. The 18th- and 19th-century owners of these burgage plots had the right to pasture animals in the Bury Field which adjoins Union Street. Their present owners still receive a proportion of the rent paid by the tenant whose animals graze the field. Domesday Book states that the burgesses had 6½ ploughs (meaning 52 oxen at eight oxen per plough) and the Bury Field may originally have been the arable land which the burgesses alone cultivated.

The Domesday picture of the agricultural potential of Newport ties in well with the present landscape. The Domesday tax assessment is low at five hides (a hide being the amount of land one family could cultivate) and this appears to have been levied exclusively on the land of five villein tenants who had five ploughs at work there. The lord of the manor's own farmland, extending to four carucates (a Danish measure similar to the hide) does not appear to have been taxed although there were four ploughs there. The villeins' houses were probably at the west end of the town where there was a green extending over several acres. Three ancient farmhouses around the green were rebuilt in the 19th century and survive as The Green, The Lodge and Green Lodge. The lord of the manor's farmhouse may also have been here as deeds to properties near the Methodist Church mention the site of the manor house. Indeed, the open pasture bordering the site is called the Bury Field, 'bury' meaning fortified place.

Apart from the burgesses and the villeins, Domesday Book lists nine serfs (the equivalent of agricultural labourers) and an unspecified number of men 'who dwell in the woodland' and paid 4s. rent for their holdings. Domesday woodland is measured in terms of the number of pigs that can feed there—300 in the case of Newport, although the woodland would also provide fuel, building and fencing materials. There was more than enough meadow land to feed the oxen which pulled the 15½ ploughs listed, for the surplus meadow was valued at 10s. The flood plain of the Ouse was and remains extensive, leaving large areas near the river unsuitable for raising crops but ideal for growing grass for winter feed. The Ouse evidently turned two water wheels, for Domesday Book values at 40s. two mills (probably under one roof) at which all the lord of the manor's tenants would have been obliged to grind their corn. The Newport described in Domesday Book is therefore a populous town with large corn mills, extensive arable, meadow and woodland, well balanced socially and well able to support itself and to earn a surplus as a market for the surrounding countryside.

Lords of the Manor of Newport

The owners of the manor of Newport were powerful absentee landlords right up until the 19th century. The family who lent their name to the town, the Pagnells, seem to have acquired Newport by marriage and it was Fulk Pagnell who, about 1100, gave land in Tickford to the French abbey of Marmoutier. His grandson, Gervase Pagnell, confirmed the grant in 1187 and gave the monks resident at Tickford the right to buy and sell goods at Newport free of market tolls. The Pagnells were succeeded by the Somery family whose estates in Newport were surveyed in 1245. There were then 53 burgesses in the borough. The market tolls are mentioned along with a seven-day fair, to commence on 18 October, recently granted by Henry III to Roger de Somery. The tenants were obliged to attend a portmote (a court to settle small commercial disputes) and a view of frankpledge (a manorial court where the whole community was held responsible for the good behaviour of individuals).

A survey, made on the death of Roger de Somery in 1273, gives a clear picture of the agricultural organisation of Newport and the part of Tickford not held by the monks. The manor house is described as a capital messuage with a dovehouse and garden. On the home farm there were 637½ acres of arable land and 66 acres of meadow. There were 29 tenants who worked on the lord's farm instead of paying rent and they occupied 31 yardlands (a measure of land roughly equivalent to 30 acres, suggesting a total of about 900 acres) plus a further 31 tenants who paid their rent partly in cash and partly in work. All tenants were obliged to provide a hen at Christmas and as 68 hens are mentioned there were probably the same number of farmers on the rent roll. There is mention of a deer park (to the east of Tickford's arable land) and of the mill and fishery.

Another Roger de Somery died in 1291 and in a similar survey he is said to have held 430 acres in the Portfield. This was the area of arable land to the west of the town bounded on the north by the river Ouse and the Bury Field, and on the south by the river Lovat and the fields of Caldecote. It was divided into three parts, one of which grew wheat, another part grew peas and beans and the third part provided pasture for the cattle of the town. Each year the crops were rotated so that the land recovered its fertility, the part which was pasture benefiting from the cattle droppings. Each farmer had a number of strips in each part of the field and ploughed, sowed and harvested at the same time as his neighbours. These strips or ridges can still be seen in some of the local fields which have not been ploughed in modern times.

The lords of the manor of Newport were invariably landed families, like the Ormonds, who played a part in national affairs. Whether by reason of such a family dying out or opposing the king of the day, the manor on more than one occasion came into the hands of the Crown. In 1542, the then owner, George St Leger, a descendant of the Earls Ormond, was induced to exchange Newport for some Crown land in Devonshire. Thus Newport and Tickford Priory, which had been dissolved in 1524, were added to a royal estate then being built up in this area. Edward VI gave Newport to his sister Elizabeth and James I gave it to his wife Ann. Eventually, in 1627 the Crown sold Newport to Sir Francis Annesley, a native of Newport Pagnell and a successful soldier. Sir Francis, who rose to become Principal Secretary of State in Ireland, was given the Irish title of Viscount Valentia, and later that of Lord Mountnorris. His son Arthur was given the English title of Earl of Anglesey in 1661. The Annesley family continued to own the manor of Newport until 1810.

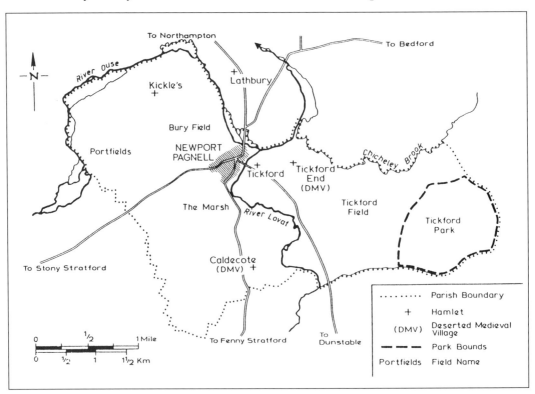

Medieval fields and hamlets of Newport Pagnell.

The Annesleys were conventional landlords and continued the medieval system of open-field farming in the Portfield until they promoted an Act of Parliament in 1794 which appointed commissioners to reallocate the land. Each farmer put in a claim based on the acreage and quality of his various strips in the fields and the value of his rights to pasture animals. The more influential claimants, like Dr. Patrick Renny of Green Lodge, were allotted a similar acreage behind their existing farmhouses, but others received a block of land in a distant part of the fields. Sir John Riddell was awarded 161a 1r 21p to the north of the road to Stony Stratford where the aptly named Newport Fields Farm was built as a direct result of the enclosure. The allotments were described in the Enclosure Award of 1795 in terms of their position in one of the former three open fields. Thus we know that the field nearest the Ouse was called Pitwell Field, the field in the centre either side of the road to Stony Stratford was called Linches Field and the field to the south west of the green was known as Green Grove Field.

Tickford

The parish of Newport includes the neighbouring villages of Tickford to the east and Caldecote to the south. Both villages are separately listed in Domesday Book. Tickford, like Newport, belonged to William son of Ansculf and had the same taxation at five hides. It is unusual in having five sokemen (tenants free from any duty to cultivate their lord's land). These sokemen may well have been English landholders who were not displaced at the Conquest, for Domesday Book records that, in the time of King Edward, five of his thegns held three-and-a-half virgates (a virgate is a quarter of a hide) and could sell the land to whom they wished. As in Newport, William's own farmland, two carucates with two ploughs, does not appear to be taxed. Six villein tenants had six ploughs between them and there were four serfs. There is only enough meadow land for five ploughs and there is woodland for only 50 pigs.

It was common in the medieval period for great landowners to give land to religious orders whose members could then be expected to pray for the donors' souls in perpetuity. Fulk Pagnell granted part of his manor of Tickford to the abbey of Marmoutier at Tours early in the 12th century. His grandson Gervase Pagnell confirmed the gift in 1187, mentioning land in several neighbouring villages, including the mill and one virgate of land in Caldecote.

At a visitation of 1233, it was recorded that the Prior of Tickford kept the rule so badly that the house was a scandal to other religious people and that the number of monks was not half what it should be. Simon de Reda, Prior in 1275-91, was deposed for 'waste of goods, evil living and homicide'. About 1311 there was a fire at Tickford which destroyed all the charters recording grants of land and privileges to the monks. A new charter was therefore obtained from the Crown, listing their holdings, including all the land on each side of Monechustret (now Priory Street), land and tenements in Hawestreet (now St John Street), lands and tenements before the gate of the house, a meadow called Castle Mede, the advowson (the right to appoint a priest) of many local churches and parcels of land in several local parishes.

Part of the original grant to the Priory from the Pagnells was the right to collect the tithes of the whole parish of Newport. Tithes were a tenth of a farmer's crop which he was obliged to give to the church. With the tithes went the duty to appoint the vicar of Newport and to provide him with a house. In 1340 the vicar of Newport Pagnell complained that the Prior, appropriately named Fulk de Champagne, had with two others besieged his house at Tickford, and broken the doors and windows.

When the vicar tried to escape they insulted, beat and wounded him and threatened to burn his house over his head if he returned to it.

In 1524 the Pope gave permission for certain religious houses to be suppressed and their revenues diverted towards Cardinal Wolsey's grand scheme for a new college at Oxford. Tickford Priory was earmarked for this purpose and a meticulous survey of the buildings and lands was made. The last Prior was given a pension and the income from letting the house and land was paid to Cardinal's College, later to be called Christ Church, Oxford. After the downfall and death in prison of Cardinal Wolsey, Tickford passed to the Crown. Tickford Priory, along with the tithes of Newport, was purchased from the Crown in 1600 by Dr. Henry Atkins, later to become the King's physician. In 1757, his family sold the site of the Priory to a wealthy local farmer, John Hooton, whose son Thomas built the present house about 1765. The tithes of Newport, Tickford and Caldecote were sold separately and were gradually purchased by the owners of the land on which they were charged.

When the Pagnell family gave land in Tickford to the Abbot of Marmoutier, they retained the bulk of the land in the village and also the deerpark on its eastern boundary. Thus the deerpark and the manorial rights to Tickford passed to the Crown with the manor of Newport. In 1600, the deerpark was sold to Sir John Fortescue of Salden in Mursley, then Chancellor of the Exchequer. When the Fortescues sold it in 1620 to Dr. Henry Atkins, who already owned the former Priory, it still had a stock of deer and a boundary wall made of stone. The Atkins family did not maintain the deer. The woodland was cleared and divided into hedged enclosures. A farmhouse was built in the centre of the park and a mansion called Tickford Park was built in the south of the park near to the village of Moulsoe. After the Atkins family estates were sold in 1757, Tickford Park had a succession of owners, eventually becoming the property of Henry Van Hagen, whose death in 1832 is commemorated by a monument in Newport Church. From the Van Hagens, Tickford Park passed to the Carringtons who demolished the house as recently as 1976, although Tickford Park Farm remains.

The manorial rights over the village and common fields of Tickford were retained by the lords of Newport. It was not until 1807 that an Act of Parliament was passed appointing commissioners to enclose the common fields of Tickford. The three fields are shown on the enclosure map of 1808 as Brook Field, lying next to Chicheley Brook, Middle Field, and Mill Field, probably named after Caldecote Mill. The surveyor laid out a new road to North Crawley, running due east for over a mile, providing access to the new enclosures. Lord Valentia, owner of the manor of Newport, was allotted most of the land between the London Road and the river Lovat. Frederick Van Hagen, owner of Tickford Park and of the tithes of the lands to be enclosed, was allotted 138 acres next to the Park. Here he built Tickford Lodge Farm to exploit the new land. Philip Hoddle Ward, who had married the daughter of Thomas Hooton of Tickford Abbey, was allotted 128 acres directly behind the Abbey and a further 75 acres below the North Crawley Road. Dr. Patrick Renny was allotted the land later to be occupied by the workhouse, which in more recent times was renamed Renny Lodge Hospital.

Caldecote

At Domesday, William son of Ansculf held the whole of Newport and Tickford but only one part of the village of Caldecote. His land there was measured at three hides and one virgate and he and a villein tenant had only one plough. His mill was worth only 8s. but there was woodland to feed 100 pigs. There is a reference, unusual in Domesday Book, to a certain knight having an additional half a hide in this part of Caldecote with half a plough (meaning four oxen).

The larger part of Caldecote belonged at Domesday to the Count of Mortain. Here his sub-tenant Alvered held four hides and one virgate with one and a half ploughs on his own land and two more used by a villein tenant and five bordars (smallholders). There was one serf and Alvered's mill was worth 7s. There was woodland for 24 pigs. Another reference, unusual in Domesday Book, is to two vavassors (another term for a knight found more in counties formerly under Danish influence) renting land here.

A further part of Caldecote amounting to two and a half hides belonged to Suerting at Domesday. His own farm was one and a half hides and two borders farmed the remainder. There was only one plough. When the three component parts of Caldecote are added together a round total of 10 hides of taxation emerges, strongly suggesting that Caldecote was a single estate when the taxation assesment was originally made.

Caldecote was a typical north Buckinghamshire settlement with a manor house, mill and tenant farmers having their land scattered in strips over the common arable of the village. The water corn mill and a piece of land was given by the Pagnell family to Tickford Priory. Some of the farmers paid their rent to the Pagnells and their successors as lords of Newport and others would lease their farms from the absentee landlord of the remainder. Today only Caldecote Farm, a farm cottage and the mill house survive and the reasons for the depopulation of the village are not at all clear. It may be that the settlement did not recover from the Black Death of 1348-49, or it could be that the landlords agreed to turn much of the arable land into sheep pasture. John White, the new owner of Willen and Caldecote, was certainly in dispute with his tenants in the 1540s for enclosing 80 acres of land, but the vicar of Newport still had some glebe land in the common fields of Caldecote as late as 1634. In 1750, Caldecote was purchased by William Blackwell, a London banker, who in 1757 bought Caldecote Mill from the Atkins family who were disposing of their property in Tickford. The Blackwells auctioned the whole estate in 1800 when all the farms had blocks of land in separate areas, showing that the enclosure of the village was complete. The present day Caldecote farm is a 19th-century building and cannot be equated with the 'Old Manor House' described in the 1800 sale catalogue, a moated site about half a mile to the east.

Newport as a market town

Of the forty or so market towns once existing in Buckinghamshire, only two, High Wycombe and Buckingham, managed to escape the control of a lord of the manor and to develop enduring civic institutions of their own. Despite its size, Newport Pagnell did not send representatives to Parliament as did much smaller towns like Amersham and Wendover. Successive lords of the manor did farm out their manorial rights but the local tradesmen never established the right to hold their own courts or to take all the income from market tolls.

The tradesmen of Newport did however gain the right to charge tolls to repair the bridges over the Ouse and Lovat and it may be for this purpose that they formed the Gild of St Mary. The gild met at the *Saracen's Head* in the High Street which had been given to the townspeople in 1483 for the maintenance of bridges, the repair of roads and relief of the poor. The gild accumulated further property by gift and bequest which became known as Town Lands and included the almshouses which stood beside the Green.

The Civil War

The great strategic importance of Newport Pagnell was recognised during the English Civil War. Prince Rupert occupied the town in the autumn of 1643 and gave orders for building entrenchments. Inexplicably, the royalists abandoned the town and parliamentary forces moved in. In December 1643, Parliament decreed that £1,000 was to be raised from the counties of Bedford, Hertford, Northampton, Huntingdon, Cambridge, Suffolk, Essex and Norfolk, 'that the town of Newport Pagnell shall be strongly fortified and furnished with all necessary provisions for a garrison'. The map of the fortifications prepared by the parliamentary garrison is surely the earliest map of Newport. It shows how the town, naturally protected by the rivers Ouse and Lovat, was to be further defended by digging a ditch 10ft. deep and a bank 10ft. high all around the built up area. The bulwarks and tenails are all named and include the Mill House Bulwark on the Ouse, the Mount Bulwark where the rivers meet, and the Tannery Bulwark between Silver Street (there called Marsh Street) and the river Lovat. The map even shows the market buildings which obstructed the centre of the High Street between the Church and St John Street. Despite fears that the royalists would return to cut off a principal supply route to London, Newport Pagnell was not besieged and the garrison was disbanded in 1645.

The status afforded to Newport Pagnell during the Civil War can only have enhanced its reputation as a refuge for travellers to the north and the presence of up to 1,200 soldiers drawn from all over the eastern counties must have radically influenced the cultural and religious life of the town. Samuel Austin, Vicar of Newport from 1631, was deprived of his living and replaced by John Gibbs, whose puritan style better suited the times. Gibbs himself was ejected at the restoration of Charles II, but he continued to preach in a barn behind his house in the High Street, thus founding the Congregational Church which remains on the same site today.

The Plague at Newport Pagnell

A census of those over 16 years of age was compiled by the established church in 1676. This gives Newport Pagnell's population as 1,032 of whom 126 were nonconformists. Adjusting this figure to include children might produce a population of nearer 2,000, but there may have been even more people living in Newport prior to 1666, when there was an outbreak of the plague which must have severely checked the growth of the town. A traveller at the time wrote that 'Newport Pagnell, in which latter, though a considerable market town, is not left above betwixt 7 and 800 people'. In the whole of 1665, only 37 burials are recorded at Newport, but in the year of the plague, 697 people were buried, 257 of them in the month of July.

Trade Tokens

No less than 14 tradesmen issued their own trade tokens in the 17th century when there was a shortage of coinage. Most of the tokens bore a symbol of the trade and the initials of the issuer, so, by reference to the parish registers, the tradesmen can be identified. William Breeden's token had a pair of scales and initials B.W.E. (William's wife Elizabeth Breeden died in 1672). John Burgis's token, also depicting scales, is dated 1668, and has the initials B.I.S. (John died in 1682 and his wife Sarah Burgis in 1686.) Josiah Chapman and John Child's tokens also bore scales and a second example of John Child's token, a lead halfpenny token, dated 1667, shows a roll of tobacco and two pipes crossed (John Child was buried in 1667). The 1667 token of Edward Cooper (E.C.) bore the Grocers' Arms. He was probably a dissenter since he was presented three times at the Quarter Sessions in 1683 for absence from church. An earlier Edward Cooper halfpenny token shows a pair of scales and the initials C.E.F. suggesting his wife's name. John Davis's token has the Drapers' Arms and initials D.I.I. for John and Joan Davis. John Davis died in 1705. Robert Hooton's token has the initials H.R.E. (He married Elizabeth King of Moulsoe in 1665.) John Norman's token has the Grocers' Arms and the initials N.I.E. (John Norman's wife Elizabeth was buried April 25th 1669). Another John Norman token has only the initials I.N. and was probably issued after his wife's death. Thomas Perrott's token had a heart and the initials P.T.E. for Thomas and Elizabeth Perrott (Thomas Perrott was buried 22 February 1678/9). James Smith's token has a man and a horse and the legend IAM: SMITH SOPE BOYLR, IN ST. JOHN STREET. An unidentified Newport token has the initials S.W.F.

Occupations of those married at Newport Pagnell 1754-1800

From 1754 until 1800, successive vicars of Newport took the trouble to enter in the marriage registers the occupations or status of most grooms and many brides. The table below places these occupations in aggregate order and gives an excellent guide to the range of trades in the town:

Labourer	203	Mat maker	4	Brewer	1
Shoemaker	43	Shepherd	4	Brush maker	1
Militiaman	36	Surgeon	4	Carrier	1
Tailor	27	Whitesmith	4	Chimney cleaner	1
Butcher	26	Bricklayer	3	Collar maker	1
Soldier	24	Horse keeper	3	Dissenting minister	1
Carpenter	21	Maltster	3	Drawer	1
Baker	20	Woolstapler	3	Drover	1
Blacksmith	20	Yeoman	3	Farrier	1
Farmer	15	Attorney	2	Hair merchant	1
Gardener	13	Bellman	2	Hog merchant	1
Glover	13	Cabinet maker	2	Paper maker	1
Miller	12	Clock/watchmaker	2	Pattern maker	1
Ostler	12	Coachman	2	Pedlar	1
Lacedealer	11	Currier	2	Peruke maker	1
Lacemaker	11	Dairyman	2	Plumber	1
Barber	10	Excise officer	2	Post driver	1
Fellmonger	9	Framework knitter	2	Printer	1
Husbandman	9	Gingerbread maker	2	Ribbon weaver	1
Mason	8	Glazier	2	Rope maker	1
Post boy	8	Grocer	2	Sadler	1
Servant	8	Leather dresser	2	Shopkeeper	1
Wheelwright	7	Millwright	2	Soot merchant	1
Draper	6	Ploughman	2	Stableman	1
Gentleman	6	Sawyer	2	Staymaker	1
Glazier	6	Stone cutter	2	Tallow chandler	1
Victualler	6	Woolcomber	2	Turner	1
Tanner	6	Apothecary	1	Waggoner	1
Chaise driver	5	Basket maker	1	Weaver	1
Cooper	5	Bookseller	1	Woolsorter	1
Breeches maker	4	Brazier	1		

Occupations of females

Lacemaker	56
Mantua maker	1
Scourer	1

The largest group in the table, the 203 labourers, would be employed on the land by the 15 farmers, 9 husbandmen, 3 yeomen, 2 dairymen and 2 graziers. The fact that the shoemakers comprise the next largest group suggests that boots were being sold in a wider market than the neighbouring parishes. The 6 tanners all marry before 1770, after which date the trade seems to have died out in Newport. There are three maltsters and, significantly, a brewer, showing that the town not only supplied innkeepers who brewed their own beer but also the tied houses of a large brewery.

The other tradesmen of a market town, the tailors, butchers and bakers are well represented, but those depending on trade on the road from London to the north of England stand out. The table includes 6 victuallers providing lodging for travellers, and 12 ostlers looking after their horses. There were no less than 20 blacksmiths on hand to shoe their horses and to shoe the cattle being driven to London markets. The 5 chaise drivers, 2 coachmen, the post driver and 8 post boys were also key personnel of this coaching centre. The constant flow of soldiers and militiamen along the road must have brought serious social problems to Newport, not least their tendency to deplete the pool of desirable marriage partners for local men. The table certainly shows the importance of the lace industry to Newport's economy. The 11 dealers would provide raw materials and a market not only for the 11 male and 56 female lacemakers married at Newport, but also for hundreds more in the surrounding villages.

Occupations of Newport men in 1798

A rather different picture of the Newport economy emerges from the lists of men aged between 15 and 60 compiled in 1798 as part of the Posse Comitatus, a county-by-county census of men and resources available to fight in the war against the French.

Labourer	123	Sawyer	4	Sadler	2
Servant	38	Surgeon	4	Bellman	1
Apprentice	19	Attorney	3	Boarder	1
Butcher	17	Chimney sweeper	3	Cabinet maker	1
Shoemaker	17	Fishmonger	3	Clothier	1
Farmer	16	Lacemaker	3	Currier	1
Baker	13	Maltster	3	Hawker	1
Gardener	11	Schoolmaster	3	Leather dresser	1
Carpenter	10	Shopkeeper	3	Officer of Excise	1
Tailor	9	Brazier	2	Postman	1
Blacksmith	8	Broker	2	Printer	1
Victualler	7	Clergyman	2	Quack doctor	1
Bricklayer	6	Draper	2	Shackler	1
Licenced teacher	6	Fellmonger	2	Stationer	1
Glovemaker	5	Gentleman	2	Staymaker	1
Wheeler	5	Grinder	2	Turner	1
Cooper	4	Ironmonger	2	Watchmaker	1
Glazier	4	Lace dealer	2		
Hairdresser	4	Miller	2		

In 1798, farmers and their labourers are just as prominent, but servants and gardeners make up a sizeable group, presumably working for the gentlemen and professional class of the town. The attorneys, surgeons and clergymen and the better off tradesmen could all afford several servants, whilst the licensed teachers (nonconformist ministers, either teaching or being trained at the theological college run by the Rev. William Bull) would also come from the upper classes. There are three maltsters listed but the brewer, Thomas Meacher, was perhaps too old to appear on the return. He is, however, shown as having 12 horses on an accompanying list of those who owned horses, waggons and carts. This part of the return shows the scale of the coaching trade as Robert Clark has 16 horses, William Payne 4 horses and 8 post horses, and, at the bottom of the list, a further 20 post horses are noted, but no owner is specified. There are only two lacedealers mentioned and only three male lace makers, but the trade, though beginning its decline, still gave a livelihood to hundreds of women in the town and the surrounding countryside.

Occupations given in the 1851 census returns for Newport

The most comprehensive guide to the social structure of Newport Pagnell is the 1851 census. The following table has been compiled by bringing together terms like carpenter and joiner under a composite heading.

Agricultural labourer	281	Printer	6	Fitter	2
Shoemaker	72	Road labourer	6	Hay dealer	2
Bricklayer	52	Surgeon	6	Horse breaker	2
Gardener	43	Coal labourer	5	Mat maker	2
Servant	41	Hairdresser	5	Millwright	2
Butcher	32	Watchmaker	5	Poulterer	2
Tailor	31	Carrier	4	Silver smith	2
Carpenter	30	Chimney sweep	4	Stocking weaver	2
Innkeeper/victualler	26	Coach painter	4	Accountant	1
Baker	24	Fisherman	4	Birmingham factor	1
Groom/horse keeper	23	Fishmonger	4	Canal labourer	1
Errand boy	20	General dealer	4	Chelsea pensioner	1
Grocer	20	Maltster	4	Cigar maker	1
Blacksmith	17	Schoolmaster	4	Drayman	1
Draper	17	Woolsorter	4	East India merchant	1
Farmer	17	Banker's clerk	3	Engineer	1
Brewer	10	Brazier	3	Gas maker	1
Proprietor of houses/land	10	Cattle dealer	3	Glue maker	1
Sawyer	10	Coach smith	3	Greenwich pensioner	1
Brickmaker	9	Coach wheeler	3	Hatter	1
Coachmaker	9	Gentleman/Esquire	3	High Constable	1
Cooper	9	Hawker	3	Hotel clerk	1
Saddler	9	Lace merchant	3	Hurdle dealer	1
Solicitor's clerk	9	Messenger	3	Inland Revenue officer	1
Boatman	8	Railway labourer	3	Leather dresser	1
Plumber	8	Solicitor	3	Lock-up keeper	1
Wheelwright	8	Straw plait maker	3	Missionary	1
Cabinet maker	7	Tinman	3	Netter	1
Chemist/druggist	7	Whitesmith	3	Parchment maker	1
Clergyman	7	Woolstapler	3	Pig dealer	1
Mason	7	Lawyer/barrister	2	Pillow maker	1
Annuitant/fundholder	6	Coach trimmer	2	Post driver	1
Auctioneer/surveyor	6	Coachman	2	Post horse master	1
Basket maker	6	Confectioner	2	Postal clerk	1
Drover	6	County Court bailiff	2	Postillion	1
Ironmonger	6	Corn merchant/mealman	2	Postmaster	1
Labourer	6	Currier	2	Postman	1
Miller	6	Earthenware dealer	2	Railway storekeeper	1
Painter	6	Fellmonger	2	Road surveyor	1

Rope maker	1	Tallow chandler	1	Veterinary surgeon	1
Shepherd	1	Tollgate keeper	1	Waggoner	1
Shop boy	1	Trunk maker	1	Whip maker	1
Stable boy	1	Turner	1	Workhouse master	1
Stone engraver	1	Umbrella maker	1		

Female occupations listed in the 1851 census returns

Lacemaker	316	Collar maker	3	Broker	1
Servant	244	Milliner	3	Cap maker	1
Dressmaker	74	Barmaid	2	Lady	1
Laundress	39	Errand girl	2	Lodging house keeper	1
Annuitant	27	Governess	2	Midwife	1
Straw bonnet maker	18	Hawker	2	Mop maker	1
Schoolmistress	15	Knitter	2	Nurse	1
Seamstress	15	Proprietor of housess	2	Upholsterer	1
Charwoman	7	Shopkeeper	2	Workhouse matron	1
Cook	6	Basket maker	1		
Straw plait maker	5	Beershop keeper	1		

The Lace Industry

Newport Pagnell's rôle as a market for cattle and provisions was far outweighed, certainly in the 18th century, by its rôle as a centre for the domestic lace industry. No account books or diaries of Newport lacemen have come to light, but we do know that, as early as 1611, cases were brought against Newport men who 'continually travelled to sell bone lace on the sabbath day'. They would supply linen thread and patterns to workers in their homes and take the product to London, where lace was worn in abundance by fashionable men and women. In 1700, Thomas Cox wrote of Newport Pagnell that 'this town is a sort of staple for bone lace, of which more is thought to be made here than in any town in England'.

Some idea of the profits to be made by lace dealers can be gained from two 17th-century inventories. When William Smyth of Newport Pagnell, a yeoman, died in 1682, he had in his house bone lace worth £84 17s. 8d., and lace thread and money in the house valued at £41 19s. 0d. A Newport Pagnell laceman called Joseph Jones had a parcel of bone lace and threads worth £10 18s. 6d. at his death in 1685. Some of the lace dealers described themselves as drapers and farmers, or even as gentlemen, and their secondary occupations do not appear in indexes to wills. Despite this limitation the following names of 18th-century Newport lace dealers have been compiled from lists of wills proved in the Prerogative Court of Canterbury, from fire insurance records and from the Universal Directory of 1792.

Allibone, Nathaniel PCC will 1731
Battenson, Thomas fire in. 1730
Baxter, Dunny fire in. 1781, Dir. 1792
Beaty, Walter PCC will 1749
Beaty, Walter PCC will 1791
Beaty, Walter dir. 1792
Black, Nelson PCC will 1711
Chapman, Thomas dir. 1792
Chibnall, John PCC will 1772
Chibnall, Robert mar. 1774, fire in. 1777,
   1782, PCC will 1783
Church, John PCC will 1767
Cleaver, William fire in. 1781, dir. 1792
Coles, Richard fire in. 1725
Cox, Henry PCC will 1777
Cran, Henry dir. 1792

Crichton, Charles PCC will 1733
Crighton, Richard fire in. 1720
Fairy, John mar. 1772
Geary, Matthew fire in. 1725
Hamilton, John fire in. 1782, PCC will 1783
Hamilton, Thomas Abbott fire in. 1783
Hanscomb, Isaac Henley dir. 1792
Hill, Thomas mar. 1776, fire in. 1777
Kunnison, Robert fire in. 1777, 1781
Lattimer, Robert PCC will 1727
Leadbetter, John PCC will 1766
Lovell, Sarah dir. 1792
Mainott, William PCC will 1755
Matthew, John fire in. 1724
Milgate, John mar. 1788
Milward, Robert PCC will 1764

Pasley, Walter mar. 1762
Pater, Thompson mar. 1763
Pawsey, John dir. 1792
Pearson, John PCC will 1780
Pearson, John mar. 1779, fire in. 1781, 1786, PCC will 1792
Pearson, Robert fire in. 1777
Percival, Edward PCC will 1763
Phillips, John fire in. 1785, dir. 1792
Purratt, William mar. 1783, dir. 1792
Robinson, Bishop mar. 1775, fire in. 1777

Robinson, Mary dir. 1792
Saxby, John fire in. 1730
Seeley, Martha fire in. 1780
Smith, Richard PCC will 1749
Smith, Thomas mar. 1768
Spencer, William mar. 1765
Stratton, James dir. 1792
Thorp, Samuel fire in. 1777
Thorp, Samuel PCC will 1787
Williat, Robert dir. 1798

It is difficult to estimate the number of outworkers employed by the town's lacemen. The Newport Pagnell marriage registers from 1754 to 1800 also record the marriages of 11 male and 56 female lacemakers but, as most wives and daughters of agricultural labourers supplemented the family income by making lace, the real number of lacemakers in the town must have been much greater. By 1851, when the trade was suffering from competition from machine-made lace from Nottingham, there were still 316 lacemakers in Newport Pagnell and over 10,000 in Buckinghamshire as a whole.

Two Newport lacemen gave evidence to the Children's Employment Commission in 1862. William Marshall employed lacemakers in an area 15 miles around Newport, meeting the workers at an inn in each village. He supplied the parchment patterns but expected the workers to buy the thread from the drapers. Some of the lacedealers had so many outworkers that they could not deal directly with all the lacemakers. William Ayres covered the same area as Marshall but dealt with intermediaries as well as his own workers. The lacedealers often supplied materials to the lacemakers who ran lace schools in their cottages. There were several of these small schools in Newport where perhaps 20 girls aged from five years would be bent over their lace pillows as long as there was daylight. Mrs Harris's lace school was visited by a commissioner who found the girls working in a hot and crowded room 'without candle after it was so dark that I could hardly see to write'.

The plight of these young workers was eased by the 1870 Education Act, which enforced attendance at schools recognised by the state, and by the rapid decline of the trade in the later 19th century. Despite attempts to revive the trade, such as the foundation of the North Bucks Lace Association in 1897, the position of Newport as a centre of a widespread cottage industry was lost for ever.

The Parchment Industry

In the 1792 directory of Newport, one Joseph Erington, a lace pattern maker, is listed. Lace patterns were made of parchment which was probably made in the Newport area throughout the period when the lace industry prospered. Gaius Hillyard, who kept the *Green Man* on the corner of Silver Street and Caldecote Street in the 1870s, ran a parchment works at the rear of the pub. Parchment is made from sheep skin and one fellmonger, or dealer in skins, David Cook, had diversified into parchment manufacture at premises between Caldecote Street and the river Lovat by 1871. This business was taken over by William Cowley & Co. who still make parchment on the same site today and are the only parchment makers left in this country.

The parchment is made from sheep skins which are stretched on a frame, scraped smooth, treated with various chemicals and left to dry in the open air for four or five days. The skins are then cut from the frames and go through further stages of cleaning and purifying before the work is complete. William Cowley & Co. also make vellum from unsplit calf skin, and their parchment was used when Domesday Book was recently restored and rebound. Much of the firm's production goes abroad.

Coachbuilding

In a town that drew so much of its income from travellers, it was natural that wheelwrights and coachbuilders should settle in Newport. Joseph Salmons established a coachbuilding works here in 1820 and made horse-drawn vehicles of all descriptions, as well as handcarts and barrows. The company began to make car bodies in 1898, one of the earliest being a Daimler for Sir Walter Carlisle of Gayhurst House. The oldest surviving Salmons-bodied car is a Silverstream, built for an Irish gentleman in 1907. The car is preserved in Ireland and is illustrated on an Irish ten punt note.

By the early part of the present century, the company was run by Joseph Salmons's two grandsons, George and Lucas. Salmons had a stand at the 1912 motor show and soon gained a reputation for high class motor coachwork, building bodies for many makes of cars and specialising in open vehicles. In 1913 the production of horse-drawn vehicles ceased. By the outbreak of war in 1914 they were employing some 350 men and electricity had been installed in the factory. At this time they opened large showrooms and repair works in St Martin's Lane in London. During the first war the factory built ambulance bodies, many of which went to the Russian front.

In 1923, the Salmons Light Car Co. was formed to produce their own car, the 'NP'. About 400 were built over the next two years, but, as the car was relatively expensive, the firm was not able to compete with larger scale producers and manufacture of the NP was discontinued. In 1926, Salmons produced a wind-down hood which could be fitted to converted saloon car bodies. The factory converted hundreds of cars of all makes; even an Austin Seven could have a Tickford hood. This conversion work helped to keep the company successful although by 1938 they were also building up to 40 bodies a week and had some 500 employees. During the war the firm was engaged in work for the Air Ministry and the Admiralty. In 1948 car manufacture was resumed with bodies for Alvis, Daimler, Healey, Humber and Lagonda. The company soon commenced the construction of caravans and had wireless contracts with the Ministry of Supply.

With the sale of the company to David Brown in 1955, production was restricted to Aston Martin and Lagonda cars, both of which companies were owned by David Brown who closed his factory at Feltham, and moved many of the workforce to Newport. Aston Martin and Lagonda have had several owners over the years and are now part of the Ford empire. They still produce high quality motor vehicles, drawing on the highly skilled local work force.

Newport and the coaching trade

Despite the ravages of the plague, Newport continued to be a trading centre for the surrounding district and a stopping place for travellers from London to the east midlands and the north of England. The principal inns, the *Swan*, the *Saracens' Head* and the *George*, stood in a row on the south side of the High Street. Even after the great improvements made to Watling Street by the engineer Thomas Telford, the road through Newport Pagnell brought as many coaches to the town as went through Stony Stratford. As many as 30 coaches a day broke their journeys to Holyhead, Liverpool, Manchester, Sheffield and Leeds by stopping at Newport.

The surfaces and gradients of the coach roads were greatly improved in the 18th century by the creation of turnpike trusts, where a group of local businessmen and gentry would promote an Act of Parliament, giving them powers to collect tolls on a certain piece of road and to apply the proceeds to repairing the surface. Travellers to Newport left Watling Street at Hockliffe and proceeded to the town of Woburn. This section of road was turnpiked as early as 1706 and extended to Newport in 1728. An Act of 1708 applied to the section of the road from Northampton to Stoke Goldington, and the length from Stoke Goldington to Newport was turnpiked in 1723. Further Acts of Parliament provided for improvements to the road through Olney to Wellingborough and Kettering in 1754, and the roads to Bedford in 1814 and to Buckingham in 1815. Turnpike collectors' houses were once a commonplace but, as they tended to jut out into the roadway, most have been demolished. A very ornate tollhouse stood on the west side of the London Road out of Newport until the 1960s.

Whilst the turnpike trustees could keep the road in repair, they had little control over the vital bridges which crossed the Ouse and Lovat at Newport. These had been rebuilt many times but funds for their repair were limited to the income from numerous charitable bequests managed by bridge trustees. The earliest bridges were probably of wooden construction but a single arch of an ancient stone bridge survives in Ousebank gardens, where it once served as a boat house. This may be the structure which was damaged by flood in 1809 and which was the subject of the following report in the *Northampton Mercury*:

> Early yesterday morning the Defiance Manchester Stage coach on its way from London was overturned upon the North Bridge, Newport Pagnell. From the overflowing of the water, in consequence of the thaw and the great rapidity of the current, several large holes had been washed out of the bridge, but at the time of the accident were entirely inperceptable, so that no blame can possibly attach to the coachman. The passengers three inside escaped with no material injury. Joseph Keates Esq. of Cheapside was the only person hurt, who received a slight concussion to the head. The coachman and guard, though precipitated into the stream, fortunately escaped without harm other than a complete ducking.

This accident led to the passing of an Act of Parliament for rebuilding both the damaged North Bridge and the South or Tickford Bridge. The new bridges, still in use today, were built the following year. The North Bridge is a single arch spanning the main channel of the Ouse just below the mill. A second bridge of three arches crosses a secondary channel which as it is on the parish boundary is probably the original course of the river. Both bridges and abutments were of ashlar stone, but the west faces have been spoiled by the widening of the decks which are cantilevered out over the river. After flood prevention works and the construction of a new weir in 1970, the three arch or Middle Bridge now crosses the main flow of water. The bridges were to be maintained from tolls and the 1810 toll house still stands between the North and Middle Bridges.

Tickford Bridge was also rebuilt under the powers given by the 1810 Act of Parliament. It is the oldest iron bridge in daily use by motor traffic. It was built by Messrs. Walker of Rotherham, and the sections transported by ship to London, then by canal to Great Linford and by road to Newport Pagnell. The stone abutments are of the same material and similar design to those of the North and Middle Bridges. The tollhouse to the south of the bridge survives but the porch, which extended into the roadway and enabled the toll collector to see traffic approaching, has been removed. Pressure of traffic in the 1960s led the county council to consider replacing Tickford

Bridge, but the construction of the Newport Pagnell bypass in 1979 has taken much of the through traffic from the town.

The third bridge at Newport is called Lathbury Bridge as it stands entirely in that parish. It spans a now dried up channel of the Ouse which the Northampton Road crossed in a ford. In 1740 the Rev. William Symes, lord of the manor of Lathbury, built a stone bridge here which was purchased by the turnpike trustees in 1757. Pedestrians used the bridge but coaches, except in time of flood, continued to use the ford. To the east of the bridge was a deep pool called Packman's Pit after an unfortunate carrier who was drowned there. The bridge was widened in brick in 1838 and the east side has been widened again in brick in recent years.

The Newport Pagnell Canal

The Grand Junction Canal was opened in 1800 and came within a mile of Newport Pagnell. A branch to the town was first proposed in 1793 and again in 1802 but the project was not sufficiently advantageous to the Grand Junction Canal Company. In 1813, William Praed of Tyringham, chairman of the Company, called a meeting in Newport to consider the provision of either a canal or a railway. 68 subscribers formed the Newport Pagnell Canal Company to build a canal from Linford Wharf to Newport Pagnell, with the possibility of extending it to Olney and Bedford. An Act of Parliament was passed in 1814 and work commenced in 1815. There was a drop of 50 feet from Great Linford to Newport Pagnell and the engineers had to construct six locks. The canal opened in 1817 and the main wharfage in the town, built on part of the former Green, became known as Shipley Wharf, after the mines at Shipley in Derbyshire, from where the narrow boats brought coal of much better quality than Newport consumers had been used to. The canal was of value to the town if not to its shareholders. It was eventually purchased by the newly formed Newport Pagnell Railway Company which closed the canal on 29 August 1864 and built a railway over part of the route. Much of Shipley Wharf remained and the former canal warehouses were served by sidings from the railway goods yard.

The Newport Pagnell Railway

The opening of the London to Birmingham Railway in 1838 killed the coaching trade overnight. By 1840 only four coaches passed through Newport Pagnell each day instead of 30 at its peak. All market towns were anxious to get onto the railway network and an Act of 1863 established the Newport Pagnell Railway Company. The new undertaking purchased the Newport Pagnell Canal, which was not very profitable, and used its route for the railway line. The railway was completed in a year and the first train, carrying ballast, ran on 30 September 1865. A passenger service opened on 2 September 1867.

Further Acts of 1865 and 1866 provided for the extension of the railway to Olney and to Wellingborough. Construction of an embankment over the Bury Field began, but the scheme strained the company's resources and the directors applied for further Acts in 1870 and 1871. By 1874 the Company was obliged to apply to Parliament for permission to abandon the extension and to sell the Newport line to the London & North Western Railway Company, which purchased it in 1875. The cast-iron bridge over Wolverton Road, with an approach consisting of several brick arches, stood unused for several years and was then demolished. The Newport Pagnell branch was used mostly by workmen employed by the L.N.W.R. at its Wolverton Works. The line was a casualty of the review by Lord Beeching and was closed to passengers on 5 September 1964. Goods traffic ceased in 1967. Little remains of canal basin or railway station as a health centre and fire station have been built over Shipley Wharf. The railway line from Wolverton has, however, been converted into a footpath.

The Newport Pagnell Tramway Company

On 27 January 1877 a public meeting in Newport considered a proposal for a steam tram service in the town. The same year the Board of Trade issued a provisional order under the Tramway Act to make the line from Newport Pagnell to Olney. A company was formed and tracks were laid from the railway station, along the High Street and north along the road-side towards Olney. The Board of Trade had inserted a clause in the Provisional Order preventing the line from running along the village street of Emberton, due to the sharp bends. The Newport Pagnell Tramway Company was unable to purchase land for the line on the south side of the village because it did not have the powers of compulsory purchase. The tramway company had to close and the lines were taken up.

Water Supply

The *Universal Directory* of 1792, in its description of Newport Pagnell, stated that 'the inhabitants are well supplied with water from the Ouse by an hydraulic machine for that purpose'. When Newport Mill was advertised for sale in 1787, the system was described as 'a newly erected water engine worked by one of the mill wheels, conveying the water by elm pipes unto a reservoir of 20 feet by 10 feet and three and a half feet deep, covered with brick and lined with lead, on oak pillars, standing on an eminence in the town, from which houses in North street, High Street and Bridge Street and North End are supplied with water.'

In 1887, the Board of Guardians, as Rural Sanitary Authority, raised a £4,000 loan for the construction of Ash Hill water works to serve the town of Newport Pagnell. Water was pumped up from a well into a water tower above. The supply was taken over in 1897 by the newly formed Newport Pagnell Urban District Council. Lathbury parish was also supplied from this source. In 1908, a wind pump was erected which could pump 25,000 gallons a day to a height of 100 feet. The wind-driven pump was demolished in 1951 after a life of almost fifty years and the site was cleared for the installation of a new tank. The new tank, holding 250,000, gallons was supplied by Messrs. Whessoe of Darlington at a cost of £92,000. Both water towers were blown up in April 1985 and the land used for housing.

Newport Pagnell Urban District Council

From its establishment in 1897 until its replacement in 1974, Newport Pagnell Urban District Council had only three clerks. Ernest Ward served from 1897 until his death in 1920 and saw the completion of the £11,000 sewerage scheme in 1903. He was succeeded in 1920 by Arthur Roberts who had began work with the Council in 1897 as an office boy and became Deputy Clerk in 1903 at the age of 18. He supervised the first council housing scheme in Little Linford Lane in the 1920s and the building of a further 30 houses in 1935 at Broad Street, making a total of 74 houses built before the Second World War. He also saw the Council expand from its original premises at 58 High Street into 60 High Street, the elegant house once occupied by the banker Richard Littleboy, which was purchased in 1940. The Clerk from 1950 until Local Government Reorganisation in 1974 was Frank Hall. He negotiated the compulsory purchase of Little Bury Field, on which the Queen's Avenue Housing Estate was built in the 1950s, and was able to fulfil a long-held ambition of the Council in buying the Bury Field in 1969. He also saw the Council move from its High Street premises in 1969 to Lovat Bank, the former home of the mineral water manufacturer Frederick Taylor.

In 1974, Newport Pagnell became part of Milton Keynes Borough and the only local forum was a Community Council. After a long campaign, the town was granted a Parish Council which met for the first time on 10 October 1985 and adopted Town Council status in 1988.

Newport Pagnell since the Second World War

Even in the late 1940s, Newport retained much of its pre-war character. The population had reached 4,000 but most of the local businesses, industries and shops remained in the hands of old-established families. The town's principal employer, Tickford Ltd., had returned to the production of cars, many of them for export. The Coales family still ran the town mill, and Taylors continued to make mustard, soda water and lemonade. James Lines still published the *Bucks Standard* newspaper, Coles and Lawmans supplied the bread and cakes and Hayllars in St John Street and Waltons in the High Street stocked the groceries. Coopers sold and serviced agricultural machinery and blacksmith Jack Bailey worked his forge in Union Street.

In 1955, Tickford Ltd. was purchased by David Brown, who moved much of his workforce from Feltham in Middlesex and used the skills of the Tickford craftsmen to produce his Aston Martin and Lagonda cars. Francis Coales and Sons was expanding to such an extent that its animal feed mill was claimed to be the most technically advanced for its size in the country. A serious fire destroyed much of Coales's mill in 1973 and the firm closed the following year. There was little new industry apart from Sogenique Services Ltd., a branch of Société Genevoise d'Instruments de Physique, founded in 1945, which specialised in the rebuilding of jig boring machines. Many locals still travelled to Wolverton to work at the railway works or at McCorquodales the printers, whilst others were attracted to the new factories in Bletchley, then benefiting from London overspill investment, or to the Vauxhall car works at Luton. Travel from the town was provided by the branch railway from Wolverton or by the two small coach firms running services to Bedford and Northampton. The railway closed on 5 September 1964 and the coach services ceased over the next few years.

The 1950s and '60s were a period of steady growth. Further council houses were built on the Broad Street estate and over 150 private houses were built in Manor Road and Wolverton Road by Davis and Rentowl of St Albans. On the debit side, the whole east side of St John Street was demolished in 1958 to widen the road between the High Street and Tickford Bridge. This range of 18th- and 19th-century facades was replaced by a dull row of modern shops and a new branch library. Tickford Bridge itself was threatened by a road widening scheme in 1967 and only saved after a public outcry. The need to widen the bridge disappeared in 1979 when a long-planned bypass was built and became the southern boundary of an enlarged Tickford Street industrial estate.

When the M1 motorway was opened in 1959, millions who had never heard of Newport Pagnell now knew it as the site of the world's first motorway service area. Local politicians forecast dramatic new development and an industrial estate was planned for the south of the town. What they did not anticipate was the plan by Buckinghamshire County Council, in response to government proposals for the development of south-east England, to site a new city next to the new motorway. Local people had never had much time for the authorities in the county town of Aylesbury and most were convinced that the plan was driven by the desire to avoid any large-scale development in the south of the county. By 1967, the area of the new city was designated and the name of Milton Keynes was borrowed from one of the small villages which the new city would absorb. In meetings held in Newport Pagnell to present the proposals for the new city, it was claimed that new building would be confined to the designated area which was separated from Newport by the M1 motorway. In the event, many of the people planning and building the new city wished to live in the established towns and villages around it. The result was a substantial expansion of housing in all the local villages and the development of Newport as a dormitory town for Milton Keynes. The town now has a population of over 14,000 and there are few fields left within the old parish of Newport.

The increase in population has done little for the vitality of Newport. The proximity of Milton Keynes has meant that most residents find their shopping and leisure requirements in the new city. In common with many an English market town, Newport has more estate agents than butchers and more restaurants than grocers. It is to be hoped that the landscape explained in the following pages of illustrations will survive current economic changes, just as it survived the civil war, the plague and the enclosure of the open fields.

1 Newport Pagnell is built on the high ground between the rivers Ouse and Lovat which meet at the east end of the town. Like Buckingham, it was probably a Saxon stronghold during the wars with the Danes. By the time of the Norman Conquest it was already a market town with a business community renting their properties free of the usual burdens of service to the lord of the manor. The church has a particularly commanding position and the castle built by the Pagnells in the 12th century must have occupied a site just to the east. The pasture to the south of the river Lovat is still called the Castle Meadow.

2 The strategic importance of Newport Pagnell was recognised during the English Civil War when first the Royalists and then the Parliamentarians occupied the town. This plan of earthworks to be built around the town was made in 1644, when the Parliamentary garrison feared a siege by the Royalists aimed at cutting supply routes to London. The survey shows the causeway on which the road to the north crossed the flood plain of the Ouse and also the market buildings in the middle of the High Street.

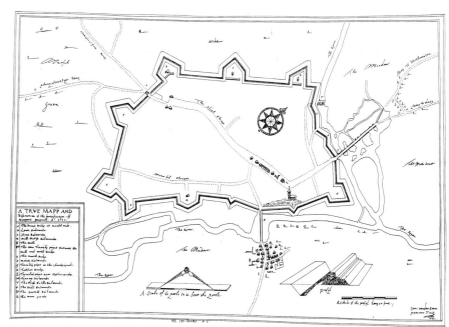

3 (*right*) The town developed during the middle ages as travellers crossed the rivers here en route from London to the East Midlands. Lathbury Bridge, shown here in 1798, was built by the Rev. William Symes of Lathbury in 1740 at a point where there had previously been a ferry for pedestrians. Even after the bridge was built, coaches were forced to cross a shallow ford which was dangerous in times of flood, and the railings mark off the deeper part of the river called Packman's Pit after a carrier who was drowned here. Lathbury Bridge was a toll bridge with a gate at either end, the owners charging a toll for crossing the bridge which was kept locked except when the river was high. Due to the increase in the number of coaches using the road, the toll bridge was purchased from Mrs. Symes in 1757 by the turnpike trustees and thrown open for the public.

4 (*below*) The original stone arches can still be seen on the west side of Lathbury Bridge. The brick parapet above probably dates from 1838 when the bridge was widened. Underneath the bridge, two joins in the masonry can be seen, one where the stone arches of 1740 meet the brick arches of 1838 and another where the more regular brickwork of the modern bridge widening is joined on.

5 (*below*) In January 1809, the Manchester stage coach was overturned on Newport's North Bridge which crossed the mill stream, at that time swollen by thawing snow. That same year, an Act of Parliament was passed for the rebuilding of the bridges at Newport Pagnell. The Middle Bridge, built in 1810 between the North Bridge and the Lathbury Bridge, crossed a secondary channel through which the Ouse flowed in times of flood. The quality of the original ashlar stonework can still be seen on the east side, but this view shows the west face which was widened with the addition of a brick parapet in 1901.

6 This view, taken from Middle Bridge *c.*1960, shows the old channel of the Ouse which formed the parish boundary between Newport Pagnell on the left and Lathbury on the right. The meadowland here has now been levelled and the old course of the river is no longer visible.

7 Major flood prevention works on the Ouse in 1970 saw the construction of a new weir and the opening out of a new channel to the Middle Bridge.

8 The bridges of 1810 were to be maintained by tolls paid by travellers on the road. The toll house between the Middle Bridge and the North Bridge still stands despite its projecting porch, which was designed so that the toll collector could see traffic approaching from either direction.

9 The Ouse was diverted to the south in Saxon times to turn the water wheel of Newport's corn mill and, until the 1970s, the mill stream took the bulk of the water of the Ouse. The mill was destroyed by fire in 1899 but the foundations remain to the north of the mill house.

10 The mill stream was crossed in 1810 by a new single stone arch known as the North Bridge. Although the parapet on the west side has been cantilevered out to increase the width of the carriageway, on the east side, the original ashlar stone remains undisturbed. To the left, one of the arches of an older bridge survives, used at one time as a boat house by the owner of Ousebank. The children are paddling at the point where wheeled traffic too wide for the older bridge would have forded the river.

11 Travellers entering the town over the North Bridge passed through an area called the North End or Bridge Street. On the right is the *Neptune Inn*, rebuilt in 1810 at the same time as the North Bridge.

12 Turning west into High Street, a visitor might choose to stop at any one of three coaching inns, the *Swan*, the *Saracen's Head* or the *George*, which stood in a row on the left of the street. The coaching trade finished in the 1840s; the *George* had closed about 1830, the *Saracen's Head* closed in the 1850s and only the *Swan* remains in business today.

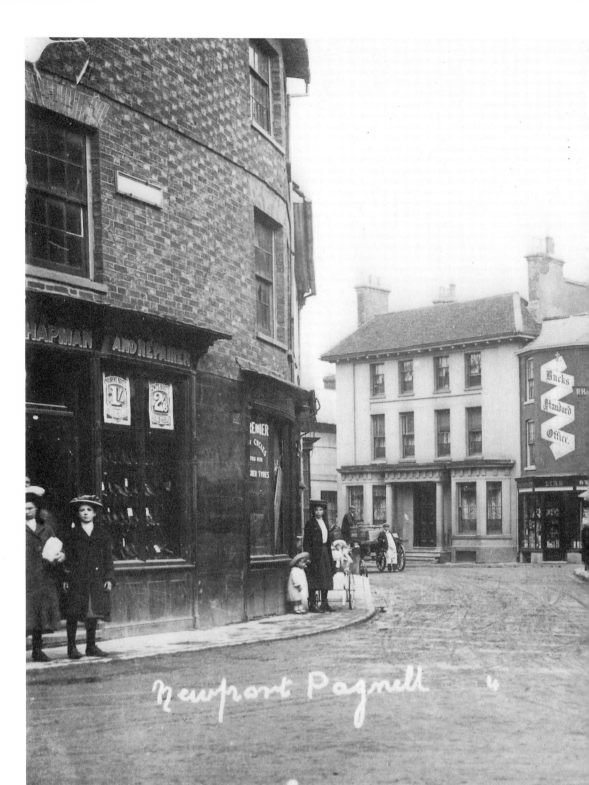

Newport Pagnell

13 The main road now turned south into St John Street which was quite narrow until the rebuilding of the left hand side in the late 1950s. The junction of the High Street and St John Street was popularly known as Cannon Corner after a cannon, probably left over from the Civil War, that stood outside an ironmonger's shop run by the Leverett family in the 18th and 19th centuries.

14 There were several inns and public houses serving travellers in St John Street. The *Marquis of Granby* was renamed the *Marquis of Chandos*, the name assumed by the son of the Duke of Buckingham and Chandos after the grant of a Dukedom to the Grenville family of Stowe in 1822.

15 St John Street led to Tickford Bridge, rebuilt in 1810 at the same time as the North Bridges. This is the oldest iron bridge in this country, and probably in the world, which is in everyday use by motor traffic. Constructed by Messrs. Walker of Rotherham, the cast sections of the bridge were shipped from the Humber down the coast and up the Thames to London, then by barge on the Grand Junction Canal to Great Linford and then by road to Newport Pagnell. William Provis was the local architect and Walkers sent down their own expert to advise on the construction.

16 In 1967, the County Council proposed the demolition of the iron bridge as part of a road widening scheme but, after a public outcry, the bridge was scheduled as an ancient monument and protected from demolition. The bridge was restored in 1989 by the County Council and repainted in its original colours. The toll collector's house on the south side of the bridge, also dating from 1810, still stands although the porch, shown projecting onto the footpath in this photograph, has now been removed.

17 Besides being a stopping point on the road to London, Newport was also on the old coach road from Oxford to Cambridge. Those travelling west would continue along the High Street to Green End. There were several inns in the High Street including the *Plough* and the *Anchor* whose porch can be seen on the left.

18 The *Plough* was a stopping point for waggons heading for Buckingham. It was rebuilt in the early part of this century replacing an earlier building of 17th-century date in front of which the local pig market was held for many years.

19 The *Anchor Inn,* whose porch extended out over the pavement, was another coaching and waggoners' inn. After the closure of the *Anchor* in 1963, the fine porch was removed and the building divided into three shops.

20 At the west end of the High Street was Green End, where several tradesmen's houses and farms surrounded a town green extending over several acres. This was the site of the weekly cattle market and the annual pleasure fair.

21 Green End, dominated by the maltings and chimneys of the Newport Pagnell Brewery Company, continued to be the site of the pleasure fair until the funfair was moved to Bury Field after the Second World War. Featured on this photograph is the carriage used to convey passengers from the railway station to the *Swan Inn*.

22 This view of Green End shows a horse fair in front of the maltings about 1914.

23 Newport's lock-up was sited on The Green. It was rebuilt about 1845 with a court room above. After the new police station was built on the north side of The Green in 1872, the building became a mission room for the Plymouth Brethren. It is now the Roman Catholic Church of St Bede.

24 Much of The Green was built up following the opening of the Newport Pagnell Canal in 1817. A new public house called the *Foaming Tankard* (on the extreme left of this photograph) was built in 1821 as were several shops and tradesmen's houses, so extending the High Street in the direction of Wolverton.

HIGH STREET.   NEWPORT PAGNELL.

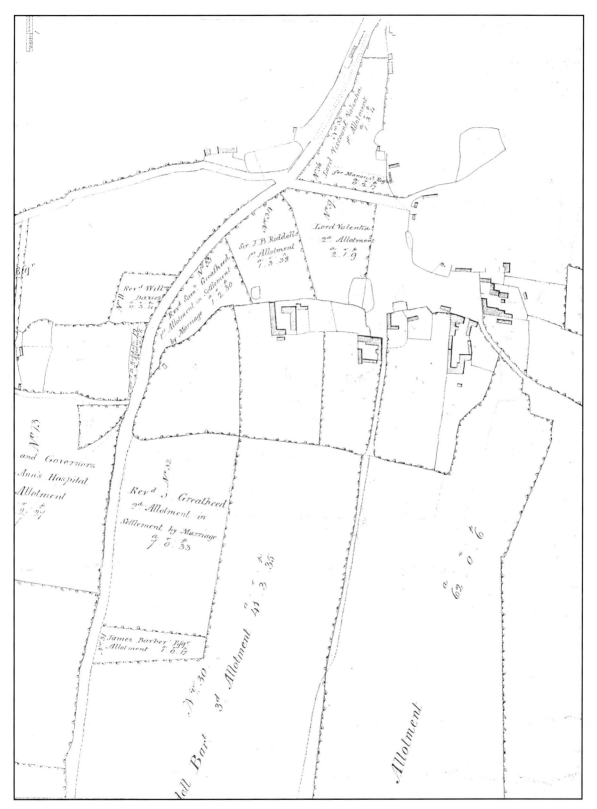

25 Around The Green stood several substantial farmhouses whose land was dispersed in strips in three common fields known as the Portfield. The Portfield was enclosed by Act of Parliament of 1794 and each farmer was allotted a single block of land in place of his strips. This detail from the enclosure map of 1795 shows that the green itself was divided among the owners of the farms surrounding The Green.

26 Only one of the farmhouses on The Green has survived. It belonged to the Price family who were farmers and corn merchants. Their farmhouse, rebuilt in the Victorian period, has now been converted into an old people's home. The dovecote is one of the few farm buildings to survive.

27 The dovecote at The Green is a listed building and is said to date from the 18th century.

28 Another farmhouse on The Green had belonged to the lace dealer Thomas Abbott Hamilton. His sister married the Rev. Samuel Greatheed, minister of the Independent Chapel at Woburn, and owner of the farm at enclosure in 1795. In the 19th century the farmhouse was rebuilt and named The Lodge. From 1850, it was occupied by a barrister named John Compton Maul and later by the Coales family who ran the nearby corn mills.

29 Newport's farmers would attend a manor court where disputes over the working of the common arable land were resolved. Another feature of manor courts was a fine imposed on farmers who failed to grind their corn at the manorial mill. Newport's medieval corn mill, powered by the Ouse, remained in use until the end of the last century. This painting of the mill dates from about 1830.

30 In the mid-19th century a steam engine was added to Newport Mill. The mill buildings to the right of the chimney were destroyed by fire in 1880.

31 Newport Mill was rebuilt after the fire as a five-storey mill with the latest machinery. It too was destroyed by fire in 1899. The miller's home is now a fine private house and the site of the mill is now part of the garden.

32 Tickford Street leads from the iron bridge through Tickford End, the remains of the medieval manor of Tickford. The buildings on the left of the street were demolished to enable road widening. The thatched house on the right, burnt down in 1945, was one of the last thatched buildings in this part of the town.

33 This sketch map of the village of Tickford was drawn up by Professor A.C. Chibnall, author of two books on Sherington and district. It shows the medieval village near the river crossing, the three common arable fields in the centre, and the lord of the manor's deer park on the east.

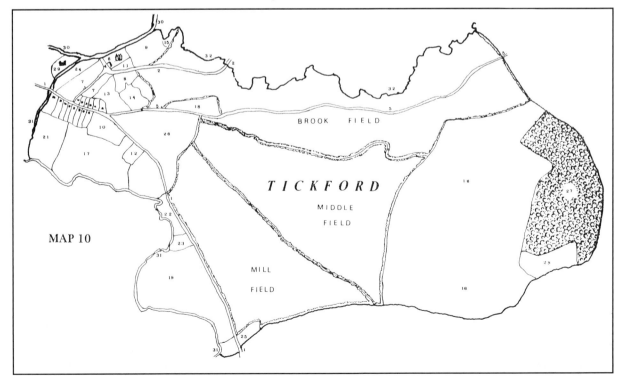

MAP 10

BROOK FIELD

TICKFORD

MIDDLE FIELD

MILL FIELD

34 Part of the village of Tickford, along with the tithes of Newport parish, was given in the 12th century to the Abbot of Marmoutier at Tours who founded a small priory here. Tickford Priory was suppressed in 1524. After a brief period during which its revenues were given to Cardinal Wolsey's new college at Oxford, it became Crown property and was sold to Henry Atkins, the royal physician, in 1600. The antiquarian Browne Willis made this sketch of the remains of the Priory church in 1703.

35 The Atkins family sold the site of the Priory in 1757 to a local gentleman farmer, John Hooton, whose son Thomas built the present house called Tickford Abbey. Several members of the Hooton family are buried in a private vault within the grounds.

36 To the east of Tickford Field was Tickford Park, the lord of the manor's deer park, which was in existence in the early 14th century when the tithes of the venison there were granted to the monks of Tickford Priory. In 1620, when the manor was purchased by Henry Atkins, it had 'its deer and stone walls enclosing it', but it had been disparked by 1757. This 17th-century house called Tickford Park was built by the Atkins family in the south of the park and was only demolished in 1976.

37 Tickford's three fields, extending over 900 acres, were enclosed by Act of Parliament passed in 1807, when the farmers of the hamlet exchanged their strips for discreet blocks of land. Enclosure provided an opportunity to extinguish the tithes (a tenth of a farmer's crop formerly paid to the church). The tithes in 1807 belonged to Frederick Van Hagen, owner of Tickford Park. He built Tickford Lodge Farm on the 138 acres of land allotted in lieu of his right to collect the tithes on all of the land enclosed under the act.

38 Caldecote Street, formerly Marsh End Lane, led to the old village of Caldecote. Although Caldecote was taxed at Domesday as a prosperous agricultural community, it was depopulated in the medieval period and its common fields broken up into a few large farms.

39 Little remains of the village of Caldecote which was situated between the roads to Woburn and Willen. Caldecote Farm, standing next the Willen Road, is a new farm built in the 19th century about half a mile west of the old village.

40 As a separate manor, Caldecote had its own manorial mill on the river Lovat. The last mill on the site of the medieval corn mill was burnt down in 1875 but this house was built in its place.

41 Newport Pagnell Church is unusually large and occupies a strategic site at the highest point in the town. The parish includes not only the town of Newport but also the villages of Tickford and Caldecote. The great length of the nave and the thickness of the chancel arch suggest that the church was once cruciform, with a heavy central tower. The present west tower was built in the 1540s and is reached not by an internal staircase but via a stair turret in the south-east corner of the nave which opens onto the roof.

42 The view of the church from Riverside is one of its most attractive aspects. Most of the old gravestones were removed from the old churchyard in 1966 when it was taken over on a 50-year licence by the local authority. Several of the more important monuments were retained, including that of the lace dealer Thomas Abbot Hamilton, who died in 1788 and whose tomb has an epitaph written by the Olney poet William Cowper.

43 Despite the size of the church, it was found necessary to build galleries in the aisles. The galleries were added in 1710 and 1724 and removed in 1926.

44 (*far left*) The nave is 94ft. by 25ft., and its fine 15th-century roof has massive moulded tie-beams supported by carved wall brackets. The roof was restored in 1935 and more recently in the 1960s at which time the carved figures were painted in rich colours.

45 (*left*) The wall bracket supporting the roof in the south-east corner of the nave has a figure carrying a shield dated 1633, probably the date of another restoration.

46 The cemetery lodge (now a private house) was designed and built by the local architect Richard Sheppard when the cemetery was extended in 1860. The funeral services for nonconformists were held in this building, which contained a chapel of rest.

47 Newport Pagnell's original vicarage still stands in St John Street next to Queen Ann's Hospital, of which the vicar was the master. It ceased to be used as a vicarage in 1875 and by 1967 the building was in poor condition. It has since been carefully restored.

48 This fine house in the High Street had been a private girls' school before becoming the vicarage in 1875. A smaller vicarage has now been built nearby and the older building converted into offices.

49 During the Civil War period, the vicar of Newport, Samuel Austin, was replaced by the Rev John Gibbs, whose religious views were more appropriate in a puritan town with a Parliamentary garrison. Gibbs was in turn displaced at the restoration of Charles II, but he continued to live in a house here on the High Street, and preached in a large barn to the rear, until his death in 1699.

50 Gibbs's house was rebuilt in the 18th century with a large archway giving access to the Independent Meeting House which his successors erected in 1702 on the site of the old barn. Newport Pagnell became an important centre of non-conformity and a surprising number of the town's wealthy tradesmen were members. The Rev. William Bull became their minister in 1764 and in 1782 began a theological college here. The bay window on the right gave light to the principal classroom. The present church was built in 1880.

51 When the new chapel was built in 1880, many of the wall monuments were saved from the old chapel and carefully replaced in the new chapel which opened in 1881. The new building seated 400 and cost £4,000.

52 To the rear of the new chapel some of the older buildings, formerly used as schoolrooms, survive. They date from the early 19th century.

53 Three generations of the Bull family served as ministers of the independent chapel. William Bull, minister from 1864 until his death in 1814, shared the work from 1800 with his son, Thomas Palmer Bull, who also lived at the house in the High Street. His son Josiah Bull joined in the work of the church from 1833 and built Bury Lawn on Union Street, where he lived until his death in 1868.

54 John Wesley is thought to have preached in the town on several occasions and a Wesleyan Methodist chapel was built here in 1815. Several cottages in the High Street were purchased as a site for a chapel and manse in 1814 by John Curtis, a lace dealer from Wootton and George Rose, a watchmaker of Newport Pagnell. The chapel served as the local circuit church until 1851. In 1888 the Superintendent Minister moved to Wolverton which then became the circuit church.

55 (*right*) The Baptists were established in the town in the middle of the 17th century. Their stone chapel, with its own small burial ground, stood on a site acquired by the Baptists in 1716. The school room, to be seen on the right of this view of the High Street, was built in front of the chapel in 1861. The chapel became disused during the early part of this century and was used for some years as a store by a local antique dealer who purchased it in 1929. In a ruinous state during the 1950s, it was eventually demolished together with the schoolroom in 1962. At that date the burials were exhumed and reburied in the London Road cemetery.

56 (*below*) During the 19th century, Newport's churchmen and the non-conformists vied with each other to provide education according to their respective codes. The National Society for the Education of the Poor in the Principles of the Established Church provided a grant for the erection of the National School in Riverside in 1816. Generations of children attended it until the erection of the Board Schools in Bury Street in 1896. After closure the building had various uses, but was in a state of disrepair when it was purchased by the Newport Pagnell Urban District Council in 1961 and demolished as part of the development of a riverside walk through the old cemetery.

57 The Infants School in Priory Street, also a National School, was built in 1867 when the school in Riverside could not accommodate the number of children in the town. Originally built for at least 70 children, the school was soon enlarged to take 100 pupils. In 1896 the building of the Board Schools in Bury Street meant that most of the small schools scattered around the town could be closed, but this school continued in use for some years and is shown here about 1902.

58 The British and Foreign School Society, founded by the Quaker Joseph Lancaster in 1808, promoted schools for the education of non-conformists' children. Dating from 1811, Newport Pagnell's British School is therefore one of the earliest in the country. The site was part of the town's Green, enclosed in 1795. The building was enlarged in 1845 but became redundant after the building of the Bury Street schools in 1896. Three years later the building was taken over by the Town Hall Company who added the red-brick end containing a stage and other offices. The Town Hall was purchased in 1939 by the Church of England and for many years served as the main hall in the town, being known as the Church House. On 1 July 1983, the building was purchased by the Baptists and was reopened as the Baptist Church in 1984.

59 The 1870 Education Act enabled towns to elect school boards which could levy rates to support non-denominational schools. The Board Schools in Bury Street consisted of three buildings; one each for infants, boys and girls. They were built in 1896 at a cost of £10,768 to accommodate 926 children. The schools fronted onto Bury Street (formerly Poole's Lane) and had playgrounds at the rear.

60 With the opening of the Ousedale County Secondary School on the Broad Street estate on the south side of the town in July 1963, the Bury Street schools became the Cedars Combined School.

61 A scene in the playground of the girls school, probably part of the Coronation celebrations in 1901. The teacher on the right is Miss Nicholson who, with her brother and sister, taught at the school all of her working life.

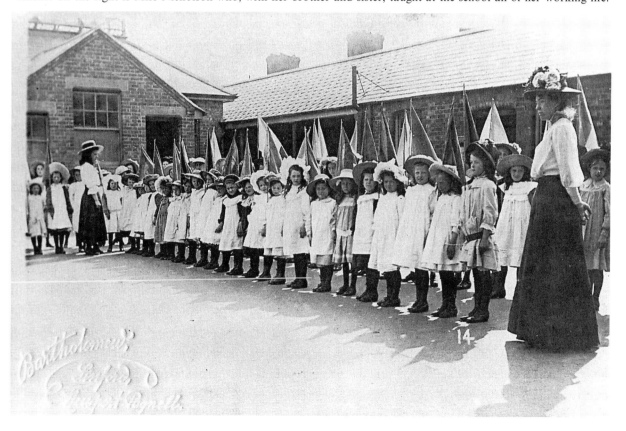

62 It was customary in medieval times for great landowners to found hospitals for the relief of the poor and sick. John de Somery, lord of the manor of Newport in the early 13th century, is thought to be the founder of the Hospital of St John the Baptist which gave its name to St John Street. Following a petition from Henry Atkins and other townsmen that the building was ruinous and no longer serving the poor, Queen Ann, wife of James I, the then owner of the manor of Newport, rebuilt the hospital in 1615.

63 Queen Ann's Hospital contained six almshouses, for three men and three women. The vicar of the parish church was the master and lived in the large stone house next door to the Hospital. This photograph shows the Hospital as rebuilt in 1825.

64 The present Queen Ann's Hospital was erected in 1891.

65 An old beam was saved from the 1615 building and inserted above the jetty of the modern structure. It has the following inscription: 'Al you good Cristians that here dooe pas by give soome thing to these poore people that in St Johns Hospital doeth ly. An. 1615'.

66 There were more almshouses in Bury Street, between the schools and the *Coachmakers* public house. These six almshouses were allocated to the poor by the trustees of the Town Lands. This view shows the Town Hall (currently the Baptist church) on the right and the almshouses at the rear on the left. The Urban District Council condemned these buildings as being unfit for occupation and they were demolished in 1945.

67 In 1755 John Revis, a wealthy London apothecary whose family came from Newport, purchased a 2,000-year lease on three cottages fronting the churchyard, demolished them, and built these almshouses on the site. He stipulated that they were to house seven old single poor men and women of the age of 55 years and upwards of the religion of the Established Church of England.

68 These almshouses in Union Street were built in 1843 by Charlotte Beaty whose father, Walter Beaty, was one of the leading lace lace dealers in the town. The four almshouses, provided for members of the Independent church only, are still in use.

69 Charlotte Beaty died in 1850, leaving in her will an endowment worth £1,700 to sustain the almshouses' charity. It is this date which is commemorated by a datestone on Miss Beaty's Almhouses.

70 More basic provision for the poor of Newport Pagnell was made by a lace dealer, Samuel Christie, who built this workhouse in 1702. He thought that it would be cheaper for the town to house its poor in one building rather than give them money to remain in their own homes. The master of the workhouse was to house and cloth them and to sell the product of their labour to defray the costs to the town.

71 Christie's concept is well expressed by the quotation from Thessalonians which was placed over the door of his workhouse: '... any would not work neither should he eat'.

72 Under the 1834 Poor Law Act, parish workhouses were to be closed and large union workhouses built in the bigger towns. The Newport Pagnell Union included 48 parishes stretching from Bletchley in the south to Olney in the north. The Union was controlled by an elected board of guardians who erected this workhouse in London Road in 1836. The adult inmates were given various activities to carry out and the workhouse children were instructed each day, their produce, such as lace and straw plait, being sold to offset the costs of the building.

73 The workhouse later became a hospital and in recent years catered mainly for the elderly. The building was closed in 1992 and demolished in August 1994. The site is to be sold for redevelopment by the Regional Health Authority.

74 The building with part timber framing at the top of Silver Street was the Church Institute, which also housed the Masonic Hall and the Working Men's Club. The Institute was destroyed by fire in March 1934.

75 The Working Men's Club moved to these new premises in Silver Street in 1902. The site had been a public house called the *Traveller's Rest.*

76 The *Swan Inn*, shown here in a painting of about 1820, is the only surviving example of Newport Pagnell's coaching inns. The inn is first noted in a document of 1597 which lists the *Swan*, the *Saracen's Head* and the *George* standing next to each other in the High Street. The 1830 directory lists over 30 coaches stopping at Newport each day; the through coaches were bound for Derby, Holyhead, Leeds, Leicester, Liverpool, Manchester and Sheffield, whilst some of the London coaches terminated at Northampton, Olney and Wellingborough.

77 The coaches could exit the *Swan* yard via Church Lane (now Church Passage) where there was a beerhouse called the *Swan Tap*. This beerhouse was tenanted for many years by the celebrated coachman, George Clarke. He took over the London-bound Umpire at 10.30 each morning and returned each night at 9.00 with the coach on its return journey to Liverpool.

78 With the collapse of the coaching trade in the 1840s, the central coach entrance of the *Swan* was converted into a lobby and access to the rear made by the demolition of the shop to the east side of the inn.

79 The *Swan* continued to be the premier hotel in Newport Pagnell. Disraeli addressed the crowds from here when he was campaigning to be one of the M.P.s for Buckinghamshire. The hotel is shown here in the late 1950s.

80 To the west of the *Swan* stood the rival coaching inn, the *Saracen's Head*, the town's major medieval inn. During the Civil War, the governor of the Parliamentary garrison in the town, Sir Samuel Luke, had his headquarters here. The inn closed in the 1850s, soon after the through coaches stopped. The building was completely destroyed in 1880 by a fire which also badly damaged the neighbouring *Swan Inn*.

81 The *George Inn*, another coaching and waggoners' inn, stood to the west of the *Saracen's Head*. When the lease was advertised in March 1802, there was stabling at the rear for 30 horses. In the 1820s, the inn was converted into a grocer's shop whose proprietor, Thomas Staines, was also the town's postmaster. The inn sign was taken by a new public house in Tickford Street.

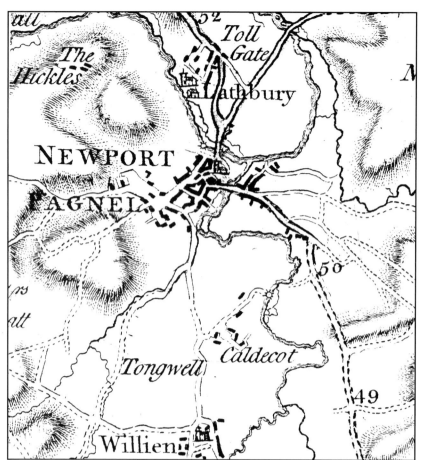

82 The speed and safety of coaches was greatly increased during the 18th century by the improvement of road surfaces brought about by the turnpiking of major routes. Jeffery's map of 1770 shows the milestones and toll gates on the road from Hockliffe via Woburn, turnpiked in 1728, and the roads from Newport to Northampton via Stoke Goldington (1723) and to Kettering via Olney (1754).

83 The road from Hockliffe entered Newport via Tickford Street. The new *George Inn* is shown in the distance on this photograph, taken about 1906.

84 Turnpike Trusts were obliged to place mileposts alongside the turnpike roads. This cast-iron mile post would have been positioned in Tickford Street about 1820 by the Trustees of the Hockliffe to Newport Pagnell Turnpike.

85 This ornate turnpike toll-collector's house stood beside the London Road nearly opposite the workhouse.

86 (*above*) The road from Oxford to Cambridge via Buckingham and Newport Pagnell was an old coaching route but it was not turnpiked until 1815. This milestone remains in place at the west end of the High Street.

87 (*right*) In 1899 a bus service, one of the earliest in the country, was established from Newport Pagnell to Olney. The two buses were Daimler cars with a special body to carry up to 10 passengers. The first bus was built by Mulliners of Northampton and is seen here at Gayhurst House on the opening day, 19 January 1899, carrying most of the founder members and shareholders of the company. The body of the second bus was built by Salmons and the two buses ran for about three years, after which the service was discontinued.

88 Regular bus services to Wolverton, Bedford and Northampton were established by 1920. Here the Northampton bus, run by the Midland Motor Bus Company, waits outside the *Dolphin Inn*. This Northampton-based company operated from 1915 to 1923 and used a Coventry-built Maudslay bus on the Newport Pagnell service. Buses on this route were later run by another Northampton firm, F. & E. Beeden, and by Hayfield Brothers of Newport Pagnell, whilst services to Bedford were run by the Eastern National Omnibus Company.

89 The motor car in turn displaced local bus services. Even in the 1920s an A.A. man was needed to direct the traffic at the junction of the High Street and St John Street.

90 The M1 Motorway, opened in 1959, relieved the pressure of north-south traffic through Newport Pagnell. The concrete bridge over the Wolverton Road is shown here soon after completion.

91 Newport Pagnell immediately came to national attention as the site of the first motorway service areas.

92 The Grand Junction Canal, opened in 1800, passed within a mile of the town at Great Linford. Inns such as the *Black Horse*, on the Newport to Wolverton road, sprang up in convenient locations.

93 Great Linford became the wharf where coal and other heavy goods were despatched by cart to Newport Pagnell and Bedford. The Grand Junction Canal Company were reluctant to build small unprofitable branches, but in 1814 prominent Newport residents formed the Newport Pagnell Canal Company to build a short branch. Great Linford thus became a canal junction. The entrance to the Newport branch is to the left of the *Wharf Inn*.

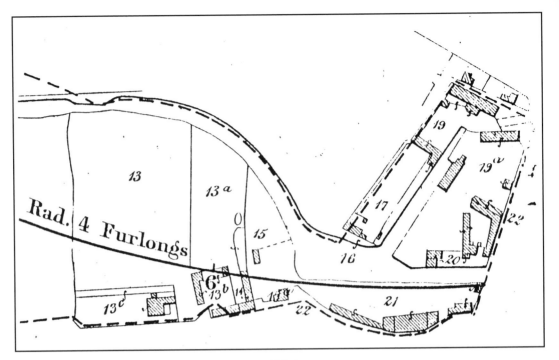

94 At its eastern end, the canal threaded its way between the farmhouses on The Green where a wharf was constructed. This 1862 map of the land required for the Newport Pagnell railway shows the various warehouses operated by the rival corn and coal merchants based at the canal wharf.

95 The canal wharf at Newport became known as the Shipley Wharf after the high-quality coal brought in by canal from Shipley in Derbyshire. These warehouses on the south of the wharf belonged to Thomas Abbot Green and Thomas John Green of Bedford whose agent, George Goff, lived near the wharf.

96 Green & Co. built a new brewery at Shipley Wharf in the 1840s. The brewery, wharf and cottage residence was advertised for sale in 1850 along with the nearby *Foaming Tankard* Inn. The buildings were later used as a corn merchant's warehouse and were sold in 1889 to Francis Coales & Son, who ran a successful animal feed and flour milling business here until their mill was destroyed by fire in 1973.

97 An arm of the canal led north from the main canal basin at Newport Pagnell to a wharf operated in 1862 by a corn and coal merchant called Gervase Smith Hives. This wharfinger's house looked south over Hives's wharf.

98 On the opposite side of the wharf was this warehouse owned in 1862 by William Price. The Price family continued to run their coal and corn merchant's business here after the canal was filled in and replaced by a railway siding.

99 These cottages stood on Wolverton Road at the entrance to Shipley Wharf. Price's warehouse can be seen through the gates. The wharf and cottages were demolished and the site used for a health centre and fire station opened in 1974.

100 The Newport Pagnell canal was never profitable and was purchased in 1864 by the Newport Pagnell Railway Company. Their new branch line from Wolverton passed through Bradwell before joining the route of the filled-in canal at Great Linford. The old canal basin at Newport Pagnell became the station and Shipley Wharf the goods yard.

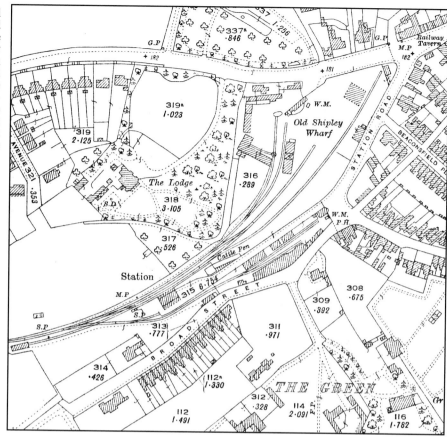

101 The station building was positioned to the south west of the old canal basin and was reached from Station Road which ran along the former canal bed between the new goods yard and Greens's warehouse.

102 Most of the passengers on the Newport Pagnell branch were local men employed by the London & North Western Railway Co. at their carriage works at Wolverton. This 'push and pull' train of the late 1940s was typical of trains operated on the line.

103 The Newport Pagnell branch was operated by the L.N.W.R., later the L.M.S. Even after nationalisation, this ex-L.N.W.R. 0-6-2 tank engine worked the branch for many years.

104 There was a minor rail crash at Newport Pagnell station in September 1959 when the 7.48 a.m. from Wolverton failed to stop in the station and ran into some stationary coaches.

105 The Newport Pagnell branch closed to passengers in 1964. The photograph shows the last train at Newport Pagnell on 5 September.

106 The siting of the railway station to the west of the town increased the value of building plots in Marsh End, despite the fact that the River Lovat regularly overflowed its banks here. The lower part of Silver Street became a fashionable place to live. The wall and a turret of F.J. Taylor's house, Lovat Bank, can be seen in this view.

107 The area between Silver Street, the High Street and Caldecote Street was developed in the Victorian period with terraced houses like these in Spring Gardens. They mainly housed the workers employed at Salmons' coachworks or at the railway works at Wolverton.

108 Wolverton Road was developed after the turn of the century because of its proximity to the railway station. Several elegant terraces were built and side roads like Park Avenue laid out.

109 It had always been the intention to extend the Newport Pagnell branch to Olney and Wellingborough and the Newport Pagnell Railway Company got as far as building this cast-iron bridge over Wolverton Road and making an embankment across the fields towards the river. The scheme strained the company's resources and in 1875 the directors were obliged to sell the line to the L.N.W.R. The bridge stood unused for several years and was then demolished.

110 There is a strong local tradition that this large Victorian house, opposite the railway station, and the pair adjacent to it, were built of bricks taken from the redundant bridge over the Wolverton Road.

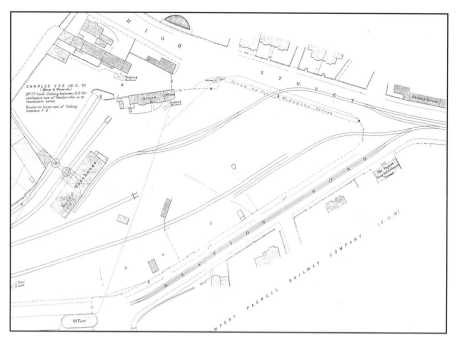

111 A further attempt at a rail link with Olney began in 1877 when the Board of Trade issued a provisional order under the Tramway Act to make a line alongside the road from Newport Pagnell to Olney. A company was formed and a large amount of 3ft. 6in. gauge track was laid. This map of the railway station made about 1893 shows the tramlines running along the High Street and Station Road, with sidings entering the goods yard.

112 This early photograph shows the tram line running down the centre of the High Street. The track never reached Olney as sharp bends in the village street of Emberton prevented the line from running down the village street and the tramway company did not have the powers of compulsory purchase to acquire sufficient land to bypass the village. Therefore the Newport Pagnell Tramway Company had to close and the lines were taken up.

113 Market towns were not only centres where farmers and merchants exchanged agricultural produce but they were also bases for the professionals like lawyers, surveyors and doctors, who served the gentry and landowners of the surrounding parishes. William Lucas was a prominent solicitor in Newport Pagnell and benefited from the enclosure of the Portfield in 1795 both as an attorney and as a landowner. He died in 1827, but his practice was continued by his son George into the 1840s. Their house, called The Cedars, still stands on the corner of the High Street and Cedars Way, the street of semi-detached houses built in the garden of the big house in the 1930s.

114 William Bateman Bull (1805-1884), son of the Rev. Thomas Palmer Bull, began to practise as a solicitor in Newport Pagnell about 1830. He built Cedar Holme on Union Street and was succeeded there by his son Walter Beaty Bull, also a solicitor. The house still stands but is now called The Manor House.

115 Market towns usually have several medical practices. The Rogers family were surgeons in the town in the 18th and 19th centuries and were staunch supporters of the congregational church. George Osbourne Rogers, son of the doctor John Rogers who owned the Newport Pagnell Brewery, lived here on Silver Street from about 1840. The house has subsequently been named Hatt House.

116 Some of Newport Pagnell's most opulent houses were occupied by the lace dealers. The trade was established here in the 16th century to employ women and children who could not find work on the land. It continued into the mid-19th century, promoted by men like Walter Beaty, a leading congregationalist, who lived at Ousebank, the large house behind the wall and gate on the left of this picture.

117 Walter Beaty died in 1791. His house is now home to the British Legion, but part of his garden was sold for an extension to the cemetery in the 1860s and another part is a public park. Newport Pagnell owes these facilities to the many highly skilled workers he employed at a time when more lace was produced here than in any other town in England.

118 Men like Walter Beaty supplied linen thread and patterns made of parchment to out-workers like this typical local lacemaker. The lace was made from numerous threads woven around pins stuck through the pattern into a pillow, which rested on the worker's knees. Hence it was called pillow-lace, or bobbin-lace, as the threads hung from brightly-coloured bone or wooden bobbins, often inscribed with the names and dates of birth of loved ones. The dealers collected the lace from the workers' homes and took it to London to sell to the milliners at the lace markets in Aldersgate.

119 Perhaps because of its use in the lace industry, parchment was made in Newport Pagnell. One of the 19th-century manufacturers was Gaius Hillyard who kept the *Green Man* in Silver Street and ran a parchment works at the rear.

120 The site most associated with the parchment trade is the factory of William Cowley & Co., where the Lovat runs beside Caldecote Street. Parchment was first made here about 1870 by David Cook, a member of the family who had for many years conducted a fellmonger's business in Tickford Street.

121 The process of making parchment involves washing and removing the hair from sheep skins, which are then stretched on wooden frames and scraped and washed repeatedly until impurities are removed and the surface is smooth enough to take ink.

122 Although Newport Pagnell was not famed for its cattle market, it did have a tannery where skins were immersed in vats of tannin at the first stage of their preparation for the leather trade. The house on Silver Street, now called the Hermitage, was the home of John Hollingworth who paid £2 4s. 0d. per annum land tax for his own house and tanyard in the late 18th century. The tannery must have been much older since part of the Civil War defences near to it were called the Tannery Bulwark.

123 Newport's corn market was not famed but the numerous local maltsters were selling large quantities of malt, either to local inns which brewed their own beer or to the London breweries. In the late 18th century, some maltsters in small towns became common brewers, buying up local inns and supplying them exclusively with beer brewed on one site. Thomas Meacher, son of a brewer from Ivinghoe, started the Newport Pagnell Brewery in the 1780s.

124 Thomas Meacher would have lived in this house between the *Dolphin Inn* and the brewery. Following Meacher's bankruptcy in 1811, and the failure of his successors, Stapleton and Baseley, the brewery was bought in 1816 by the local doctor, John Rogers, who moved into the big house, whilst a relative, Jesse Parsons, ran the brewery. Jesse Parsons and Thomas Parsons, who ran the Lion Brewery at Princes Risborough, both came from St Albans where the Parsons family were supporters of the Spier Street Congregational Church.

125 John Rogers' son, also called John, became a partner in the brewery, but died in 1856. His family sold the brewery and public houses in 1875. They were purchased by Messrs Allfrey & Lovell, the locally based partner, Francis Allfrey, later living at Bury Lawn. In 1899 the firm became a limited company known as the Newport Pagnell Brewery Co., but was taken over in 1919 by Charles Wells & Co. of Bedford. The new owners closed the brewery but retained many of the tied houses including the *Dolphin*.

126 The brewery premises were purchased in 1924 by W.J. Cooper, a manufacturer and supplier of farm machinery. W.J. Cooper & Co. made successive alterations to the old maltings. Here the lower part of the wall facing the High Street has been pierced by sets of garage doors.

127 By the 1960s the maltings had been converted into a showroom.

128 This photograph of the old brewery was taken from Queen's Avenue in 1990. The following year, the premises were sold by Coopers and an office and shop development was built on the site. In 1995, the vacant offices were converted into the Newport Pagnell medical centre.

129 There are many other sites in Newport Pagnell where the malting trade has been carried on. Rogers's brewery owned the public house on St John Street called the *Admiral Hood* (the double-fronted building with two dormer windows). Behind the inn there was a malting still in use in 1875.

130 The maltings behind the *Admiral Hood* were later used by John Odell for repairing agricultural machinery and in more recent years became a dairy which survived until the 1950s when it was demolished along with the whole east side of St John Street. Here the maltings are the scene of a civil defence exercise in 1959.

131 Rogers's Brewery also owned the *Kings Arms* on Tickford Street. This too had maltings to the rear which were in use in 1875.

132 The *Kings Arms* is shown here awaiting demolition in 1973, with the old maltings clearly visible on the left.

133 Most of Newport's inns were old-established concerns, but Rogers & Co. did build new premises in growing parts of the town such as the *Beehive* in Priory Street, first licensed in 1864, erected on the site of the *Jolly Gardeners*, which was burnt down in 1863.

134 A close rival to the Newport Brewery Co. was William Hipwell's Olney Brewery which owned several licensed houses in Newport Pagnell. William Hipwell ran the *Bull Inn* at Olney and got a foothold in Newport in 1854 by buying a small brewery started by James Price Coles behind these houses near Tickford Bridge. Coles died in 1879 and a row of cottages was built on the brewery site in the 1890s.

135 By 1862, Hipwell's were renting an old malting in Silver Street, run in the 18th century by the Hoddle family and purchased in 1796 by a maltster named Joseph Redden. In 1862 it had a doorway at the rear linking it to the same company's *Anchor Inn* on the High Street. The malting was later used by the Newport Pagnell Brewery Co. and was demolished in 1967 for the erection of a telephone exchange.

136 By 1872, Hipwells owned 10 public houses in Newport, including the *Neptune Inn*, near the North Bridge.

137 One of Hipwell's newly built pubs was the *Red Lion*, built on Caldecote Street in 1867. It is seen here during the floods of 1908.

138 Even the Unionist Club on St John Street served Hipwell's ales. This house had belonged to a solicitor called George Cooch, best known as the clerk and solicitor to the Newport Pagnell Canal Company from its inception to its closure.

139 The Unionist Club was rebuilt after a fire in 1912. This photograph shows the interior of the club in 1913.

140 Hipwell's also owned the *Coachmaker's Arms* at Green End. The Olney firm was eventually taken over by the Northampton brewery of Phipps & Co.

141 Another old inn with its own maltings and brewery was the *Bull Inn* on Tickford Street.

142 The *Bull* had been taken over by Phipp's of Northampton by 1872 when a printed list of licensed premises in the whole county was published. The group outside are coachbuilders from the nearby Salmons' works.

143 Another local brewery was started by John Wilmer, a farmer from Gayhurst, who was backed by Lord Carrington. He took over these shop premises in the High Street about 1860, set up the brewery in the yard at the back and ran the shop as licensed premises known as *The Vaults*. The brewery became known as the Cannon Brewery as it was opposite Cannon Corner.

144 Wilmer & Sons rented maltings behind the *March of Intellect* in Silver Street. This was owned by John Price Coles, the former maltster who had set up his own brewery beside Tickford Bridge.

145 When the maltings behind the *March of Intellect* were burnt down in 1876 the roof was thatched. The maltings were evidently rebuilt and became part of the Urban District Council Yard.

146　A traction engine pulling a brewery wagon outside the Cannon Brewery about 1910.

147　When the founder's son, John Robert Wilmer, died in 1904, the brewery was sold to Edgar Warman, who sold it on to the Aylesbury Brewery Company. The driver of the brewery lorry is Frank Rutter, a Wilmers' employee who later worked for A.B.C.

148 Along the High Street were the premises of T. and F.J. Taylor (Newport Pagnell) Ltd., running back through this yard to Union Street. The firm was founded in 1830 by William Taylor who made soda water and later table waters and cordials, using water from a well on the premises. Following his success with these products William perfected a recipe for mustard which was equally, if not more, successful.

149 Lovat Bank was built in 1877 for Frederick James Taylor, one of William's two sons. It was designed by the well-known Stony Stratford architect, Edward Swinfen Harris. It is without doubt the finest building of its period in the town. The house remained in the ownership of the Taylor family until 1959 when it was sold to the Territorial Army. Ten years later it was purchased by the town's Urban District Council and in 1974, with the reorganisation of local government, it passed to the Milton Keynes Borough Council. It has recently been listed as a building of architectural and historic interest.

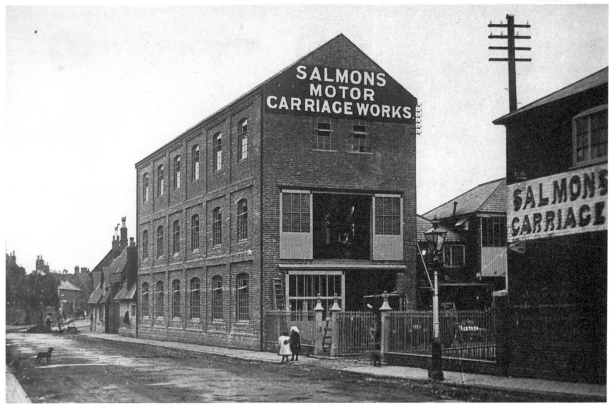

150 This elegant factory was built by the firm of Salmons and Sons which was established at Newport Pagnell by Joseph Salmons in 1820. The firm made carriages and horse-drawn vehicles of all descriptions as well as handcarts and barrows.

151 This cart was built by Salmons for the local baker, William Cole, and is shown outside Cole's bakery at 43 Tickford Street.

152 Salmons began to make bodies for motor cars in 1898, and by 1914 they were employing 350 men. From 1923-5, Salmons produced their own car, the NP. Almost 400 were made but the project was not profitable and production was discontinued. More successful was the 'Tickford Hood', which could be wound down with a handle, and was fitted to several thousand saloon cars which the firm converted to open tourers.

153 (*above*) By 1938 Salmons had some 500 employees. These houses in Tickford Street were built by Lucas Salmons and let to members of the workforce.

154 (*above*) In 1812 a bank was established at Leighton Buzzard by a Quaker businessman, Peter Bassett, who opened a branch in Newport Pagnell in 1820. In 1864 Richard Littleboy, a Quaker and a former miller, was admitted to the firm as the resident partner at Newport Pagnell, residing in the large house known as 60 High Street. Littleboy continued the bank in the original premises further down the High street until their demolition and replacement by the present building in 1870. Littleboy died in 1895 at the age of 75 and in 1896 Bassett's Bank was taken over by Barclays. The bank has recently been listed as a building of architectural and historic interest.

155 (*left*) The town's Co-operative Society was established in 1867 and their first shop, only recently closed, was at the bottom of Silver Street. The company moved to these premises in the High Street about 1920 and the new shop front was added in 1936. The Society was taken over by the CWS South Midlands Retail Group in 1994 but this is still the Co-op's main shop in the town.

156 In 1912, the proprietors of Salmons' coachworks, in partnership with local businessman Alfred Bullard, purchased a private house at the top of St John Street and built a cinema in the rear garden. The Electric Theatre was opened on 20 December 1912. Harry Bardett, the foreman engineer at Salmons, operated the equipment and made the flashing sign for the cinema.

157 The building was refurbished and renamed the Electra Cinema before 1939. The cinema, which could seat 400 people, celebrated its 70th anniversary on 12 December 1982. It finally closed in 1988 and has been converted into an arcade of shops.

158 Most small towns were lighted by gas from the 1830s and '40s. The enterprising businessmen of the town founded the Newport Pagnell Gas and Coke Company in 1837 with a gasworks in Caldecote Street. The town's gas works continued to produce gas until the 1950s.

159 The Newport Pagnell Gas Company was taken over by the East Midlands Gas Board. The gas holders were dismantled in 1968.

160 (*above*) The Police Station was built in 1872 with a court room, magistrates' room, cells for the prisoners and a house for the police inspector. In 1963, the Police Station was modernised and a new magistrates' court was provided.

161 (*right*) The town fire brigade was founded in 1855 and had 24 members. The first captain was Richard Sheppard, the local architect and surveyor. In 1888 a new fire station was opened in the High Street. This photograph was taken about 1905 when the brigade was taken over by the Urban District Council.

164 Newport Mill was completely destroyed by the fire but the brigade were successful in preventing the spread of the flames to the mill house.

162 (*above left*) In 1912, the brigade purchased a Merryweather steam fire engine. It was first used at the fire at the Unionist Club, St John Street, in 1912, when the new fire pump was stationed on the Iron Bridge to draw water from the River Lovat. After this event the pump, which still survives and can be seen in the Stacey Hill Museum at nearby Wolverton, was called the 'Lovat'. A new fire station was built by the County Fire Brigade at Wolverton Road in 1974.

163 (*left*) Perhaps the most dramatic fire attended by the Newport Fire Brigade was that at Newport Mill on 9 February 1899. The modern five-storey mill of Rowlatt & Co., completely rebuilt after a fire in 1880, was found to be on fire by the workman arriving to start the machinery. The fire was fanned by high winds and the flames were reflected in the flooded River Ouse running underneath the mill.

165 Newport Mill was the source of the town's first water supply. When advertised for sale in 1787, it was said to include a water engine which pumped water to a reservoir in the highest part of the town, from where pipes conveyed it to over 100 houses. The Newport Pagnell Rural Sanitary Authority, a health committee of the Board of Guardians meeting at the Workhouse, erected this water tower on Ash Hill, at the top of Lakes Lane, in 1888. Water was pumped into the tank by a gas engine from a well below the structure. It supplied the whole of the town as well as Lathbury parish.

166 From 1897, the water supply was the responsibility of Newport Pagnell Urban District Council. In 1951, a new tank holding 250,000 gallons was ordered from Messrs Whessoe of Darlington at a cost of £92,000. Both water towers were blown up in April 1985 by the developer of new houses planned for the site.

167 The Rural Sanitary Authority was replaced in 1897 by a Rural District Council for the villages and an Urban District Council for Newport Pagnell. The U.D.C. offices, the building with the rounded hood over the front door, were opened in 1897. The railings just visible on the left were around the house of the banker, Richard Littleboy, whose house was taken over as council offices in 1940.

168 Newport Pagnell U.D.C. occupied 60 High Street as council offices from 1940-1969. When the offices were moved to Lovat Bank, the Council intended to demolish the old building but it is a listed building and has since been restored. The small side entrance on the left, with the attractive door and window, has not survived.

169 Newport Pagnell U.D.C. moved in 1969 to Lovat Bank, an impressive house built for the mineral water manufacturer, Frederick James Taylor. With the demise of the Urban District Council in 1974, the building passed to the Milton Keynes Borough Council and is currently let as offices.

170 The Urban District Council built several small estates of council houses around the town. These houses in Queen's Avenue were built by the local builders, H.W. Mason and Sons, in the early 1950s. The council's largest estate, built between the wars, centred on a new road to the south of the railway station called Broad Street.

171 In the 1950s, with the M1 motorway being planned and traffic congestion in the town increasing, the Urban District Council discussed with the County Council several schemes for widening St John Street. The decision to demolish the whole of the east side was most unfortunate, especially in view of the fact that a bypass plan had existed since 1933 and was subsequently implemented. The *Admiral Hood* and all of the houses and shops on the right of this photograph were demolished in 1958.

Bibliography

Bale, R.F. (ed.), *Buckinghamshire parish registers. Marriages*: Vol 9, Newport Pagnell etc. (1923)

Bristow, R., *Newport Pagnell postmasters* (n.d.)

Buckinghamshire Record Office: Bull, Solicitors, Newport Pagnell: interim catalogue of deeds (1976)

Bull, F.W., *History of Newport Pagnell* (1900)

Cole, N.T. & Dawson, W., *Echoes of the past from Newport Pagnell and neighbourhood* (1968)

Coleman, D.M., *A short history of Newport Pagnell Methodist Church* (1965)

Hurst D., *The ancient buildings of Newport Pagnell* (1991)

Hurst, D., *From Marsh Street to Silver Street* (1988)

Hurst, D., *St. John Street —the cradle to the grave* (1989)

Lewis, M., *The chantry and parish gilds of medieval Newport Pagnell* (1992)

Lewis, M., *Tickford Priory: a Benedictine tragedy* (1993)

Lipscomb, G., *History and antiquities of the County of Buckingham* (4 vols., 1847)

Martin, R.G., *The Chapel 1660-1960: the story of the Congregational Church, Newport Pagnell* (1960)

Newport Rural District Council: Diamond Jubilee 1894-1954: a record of activities

Page, W. (ed.), *Victoria History of the County of Buckingham* (4 vols., 1905-1927)

Parker, A. W., *The Woburn toll road, 1728-1860* (1975)

Ratcliff, O., *History and antiquities of Newport Pagnell Hundred* (1900)

Ratcliff, O. (ed.), Ratcliff's Newport Almanac (1900)

Robinson, J., *The evolution of the townscape of medieval Newport Pagnell* (1975)

Simpson, B., *The Wolverton to Newport Pagnell branch* (1995)

Simpson, J., *History of the town of Newport Pagnell and its neighbourhood* (1868)

Staines, J., *History of Newport Pagnell and its immediate vicinity* (1842)

Tibbutt, H.G. (ed.), *The letter books of Sir Samuel Luke, 1644-45, Parliamentary Governor of Newport Pagnell* (1963)

West, V., 'Aspects of parochial poor relief in Newport Pagnell 1140-1930' (Thesis, 1974)

Index

Roman numerals refer to pages in the introduction, and arabic numerals to individual illustrations.